# Blackburn's Old Inns

First published as "*Old Inns & Coaching Houses with other vanished scenes of Blackburn*" in 1970 by The Blackburn Times newspaper. 

ISBN: 1 872895 14 X

Cover illustration
by
Brian Ormerod

Landy Publishing have also published:-

*Blackburn & Darwen A Century Ago* by Alan Duckworth

*The Blackburn Samaritan* by Trevor Moore

*Bits of Old Blackburn* by Chas Haworth, J.G. Shaw and Wm. J. Hulme

Landy Publishing
3 Staining Rise
Staining
Blackpool FY3 0BU
Fax/Tel: 0253 886103

Printed and bound by Galava Printing Company Limited,
Nelson, Lancashire

# Blackburn's Old Inns

by

George Miller

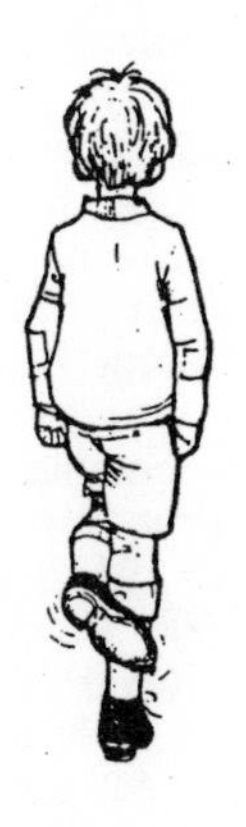

Landy Publishing
1993

# Foreword

**by Stanley Miller**

*'Blackburn's Old Inns'* is an example of a more light-hearted approach to local history, and covers an era when Blackburn's numerous inns and taverns formed the focal point for much of the town's social life. Since those splendid days their ranks have been seriously depleted by the endeavours of the temperance lobby, population displacement, and town centre redevelopment. In view of these social changes it is appropriate that a reprint of the booklet should appear.

The author, my father, was born at 122 Haslingden Road in May 1897, being educated at the Public Higher Grade School with a view to a clerical career. The outbreak of the First World War brought short a period of employment in the Blackburn Corporation Gas Department, and May 1915 found him enlisting in the Royal Field Artillery. He saw service on the Western Front at the Somme, Ypres, and St. Quentin, where he was wounded during the retreat of March 1918. After convalescence, he was appointed Gunnery Instructor at Preston Park, Brighton.

On demobilisation, he joined his father's heavy haulage business, but this was wound up in the slump of 1930. After some ventures in the printing trade, including the launching of a short-lived weekly newspaper, the *'Colne and Nelson Advertiser'*, George Miller became a Civil Servant until his retirement in November 1963. During his public service career, he won the Vansittart Prize for a first novel in a competition organised by the Civil Service Authors Society. The novel was a historical romance set in Britain during the Roman occupation. The background research stimulated an interest in local history, the first fruit of which was a *'History of Hoghton Tower'* published in 1948 after several years work in the County Record Office. Over the next few years, four books on the history of Blackburn were published, as well as several pamphlets, and numerous articles in the *Evening Telegraph* and especially the *Blackburn Times,* to which George Miller contributed for over 30 years.

In addition he was a keen member of the Lancashire Authors' Association, winning the Pomfret Cup for Lancashire Dialect Prose in four consecutive years, from 1954 - 1957. This interest in dialect eventually resulted in over 500 short stories for the *Lancashire Evening Post* and *St. Helen's Reporter.*

After his retirement he took up a post as Honorary Curator of Rufford Old Hall, which he held for almost ten years.

He married Miss Mary Elizabeth Bolton in May 1922. She died in October 1975. There were two children, John a retired Master Mariner and James Stanley a retired Librarian. George Miller died in August 1981.

# INTRODUCTION

Within the past two decades almost all of Blackburn's ancient hostelries, many with associations reaching back as far as the 17th century, have been swept from the face of the earth. Their foundations are now straddled by the nucleus of a futuristic Blackburn of steel and concrete, austere, imposing and impersonal, gleaming white above the ruins of the old order, portentous and, to many, vaguely menacing. The industrial revolution, itself sufficiently revolutionary, is making way for the electronic age and all that it implies.

Standing at the junction of Church Street and Victoria Street, within an area of a few acres, one can see the sites of no fewer than twelve old inns that have been swept into oblivion.

The names of some, such as the Black Lion in Shorrock Fold, the Eagle and Child at the top of Darwen Street, the New Bull in Fleming Square and the Freemason's Arms in Salford, have long been forgotten, even by the older generation, but others, such as the Old Bull and the Golden Lion in Church Street, the New Inn in Victoria Street and the Bay Horse in Salford, still bring back nostalgic memories to those who recall the Blackburn of bygone days.

Almost all of these grand old inns were places of character, as were the men and women who acted as mine host down the centuries. Many were coaching inns, posting stations or depots for carriers' wagons and others had rooms set aside for public meetings and assemblies, balls, waxworks exhibitions, itinerant companies of play-actors and the like. Some, like St. John's Tavern, had a snug little sanctum reserved for churchwardens' meetings and others were the headquarters of innumerable societies.

Throughout the years they have watched the colourful pageant of civic life throng past their thresholds in all its aspects of pomp and circumstance, of poverty and squalor. They have seen changes in fashions of thought and of dress and the structure of more than one political system created and destroyed.

They have seen the tempo of life falter or quicken, like the pulse of a mighty heart, as the wheels of industry slowed or accelerated by the ebb and flow of trade. They have seen the handloom displaced by the power loom and the stage coach give way to the motor car; indeed, it is not too much to say that the scenes they have witnessed might well provide material for an epitome of the cotton trade.

We sometimes overlook the fact that these old hostelries played a far more active part in the social life of the community than do their modern counterparts. They were in a large measure self-contained units, each brewing its own ale, making its own bread, cheese and butter and often slaughtering its own cattle and pigs. In addition mine host usually kept a well-filled stable, supplying post-horses and post-chaises to travellers, draft horses to local carriers and often driving a stage or market coach himself.

The inn also acted as a sort of clearing-house for the transport of goods and merchandise. Here letters were collected and delivered, messages transmitted and news circulated. Here quack doctors and strolling players congregated for the well-being and enlightenment of the populace, whilst every form of local activity, whether social or commercial, was encouraged.

Here an attorney might interrogate a prospective client in a cosy back room, two cotton merchants might clinch a deal or a "putter-out" might come to terms with some anxious handloom weaver.

Students of Georgian or early Victorian times are often surprised at the relatively large number of inns and hostelries per head of population as compared with the present time, overlooking the fact that tea as a beverage is of comparatively recent origin and that in those bygone days ale was the staple drink.

Even well or spring water was suspect, being often impregnated with the drainage of privies or sewers, so that the very children were given a drink composed of an infusion of herbs made safe by boilings.

But many years ago Blackburn was once stigmatised by the Rev. J. Clay, chaplain of Preston House of Correction, as "the most beery town in the world." In his annual report he stated roundly that: "There is a greater proportion of the uneducated classes in Blackburn than in Preston and the passion for liquor is a source of ruin and disgrace more fruitful than every other source combined. Between July Sessions 1831-3 there have been committed for trial on charges of felony sixty-eight persons from Blackburn."

The statement is, of course, wholly libellous. What the reverend gentleman failed to appreciate was that the two towns were (and still are) of an entirely different character.

At the beginning of the last century, Preston was the home of a leisured professional community, being the centre of the county's civic administration. In addition, many of the landed gentry had a town house in the borough.

Hence, it is not surprising that Blackburn, purely a manufacturing town, should have a larger percentage of illiteracy among its cotton operatives, many of whom were treadling a handloom at the age of ten.

But if the charge of illiteracy can be sustained, this by no means implies that drunkenness was one of its concomitants. On the contrary, handloom weavers were hard pressed to keep body and soul together, let alone waste their scanty substance on riotous living. It was rather the well-to-do gentry and the professional classes who maintained the hard-drinking tradition of the Regency period, when to be "a three-bottle man" was a coveted distinction.

The essential difference between a drunken Preston lawyer and a drunken Blackburn weaver was that the former had his own cellar and drank at home, whereas the latter went to the public ale-house and so became the legitimate prey of the constable and the watch. Had the clerical critic taken the trouble to collect a few statistics, he might have modified his opinion.

Here are some statistics from Baines' History of Lancashire, published in 1824. Blackburn, with a population of 53,350 inhabitants, had 77 hotels, inns and taverns, while Preston, educated and law-abiding Preston, had no fewer than 81 to a population of 27,300, about half that of its much-maligned neighbour. Further afield, we find Bolton, of 50,197, had 96 hotels, inns and taverns, whilst Wigan had 68 to a population of 38,318.

So much for "beery Blackburn." On these figures, the township might well have claimed the title of sober Blackburn.

*The north end of old Northgate, drawn from the pavement of the Mason's Arms, now the site of the Co-op Emporium*

CHAPTER 1

# Northgate, a Street of Inns

I SOMETIMES wonder if it is just a coincidence that Northgate, once known as Blackburn's street of inns, and doubtless the scene of innumerable clashes between drunken rowdies and the forces of law and order, should now be our Police Headquarters. Those of us who still remember Blakeley Moor in its unregenerate days, will surely see something of deeper significance in such a transformation.

It is widely assumed that our English hostelries had their origin in the ancient Tabernae or rest-houses erected by the Romans on the line of their military roads. In the Middle Ages these were identified by a holly or ivy bush suspended over the doorway, insignia later replaced by painted signs, usually with some local significance, such as the arms of the lord of the manor.

Blackburn's oldest inn signs seem to give the Bull pride of place, possibly because that ferocious beast was the crest of the de Hoghtons, of Hoghton Tower. We have had Old Bulls and New Bulls, Black Bulls and White Bulls, Bull's Heads and at least one Bull and Butcher, a corruption of Boleyn Butchered, alluding to the grim fate of Anne Boleyn, Henry VIII's second wife, who died on the scaffold.

Other inn signs within the township included two Red Lions, two Dukes of Wellington, two Lord Nelsons and two Jolly Dragoons, one of which was formerly tenanted by the inventor John Osbaldeston as licensee for some time.

In addition we had such quaint and curious gems as Mother Red Cap, Utick's Nest, Who could ha' thowt it, New Drop, Flowing Jug, Gaping Goose, Sweet Willow, Stop an' Rest, Hole i'th Wall, Doctor Syntax, Turk's Head and Blackamoor.

Of these, Mother Red Cap was a cant name for an old ale-wife ; the original Utick was a bird called the stonechat, while the inn so-called was a favourite haunt of reachers-in from neighbouring factories. colloquially known as Uticks from the squatting position they adopted at work, resembling that of the bird on its nest.

The New Drop has a sinister gallows flavour for which there is no accounting, but I believe the Gaping Goose to have an ecclesiastic origin.

Its ancestor may still be found in many an old church carved on bench ends or rood screens or misericords by medieval craftsmen in the form of a device known as "The Pelican in Piety." According to legend this bird feeds its young with its own blood and so was chosen by the early church as an example of self-sacrifice. Similarly, Doctor Syntax was an 18th century character made famous by Rowlandson's illustrations, whilst both Turk's Head and Blackamore derive from devices born by knights on their shields during the Crusades.

Be all this as it may, there is no doubt that in 1822 Blackburn had no fewer than 77 such signs swinging over its cobbled streets to attract the eye of the weary, not to say thirsty traveller. Of these Northgate had no less than 15, Darwen Street had 11, Church Street had eight and King Street, five. On Northgate's quota, all but two have gone, although several newcomers have taken their place. But the citizen of yesteryear would look vainly for the Joiner's Arms (later called the Paganini), which stood at the corner of Higher Cockcroft; the King's Arms, which stood two doors further north; the Black Horse, which was between New Market Street and Engine Street; the Jolly Sailor, which stood at the corner of Cannon Street; the Red Lion two doors further north; the Punch Bowl, the Boar's Head and the General Wolfe, all between Cannon Street and Duke Street; and on the other side of the thoroughfare the Mason's Arms, which stood at the corner of Thunder Alley, where the Co-op Emporium now stands; the Nag's Head and the Holy Lamb (later the Stanley Arms), between New Market Street and Lord Street, with the Black Greyhound and the Dog and Duck between Lord Street and Church Street.

In the diary of the Rev. Peter Walkden, Noncomformist minister of Chipping, there is an entry dated 1725 alluding to the King's Arms in Northgate, where Thomas Entwistle and he "had two pots of cider."

Peter was quite a character and not averse to profiting by the needs of his flock. Having organised a regular pack-horse train from Eccleshill coal pit across country by way of the Roman road over Blackamoor and Whinney Edge, via Brandyhouse Brow to Northgate and Shire Brow and so on to the valley of the Ribble by way of the ford at Ribchester, he purchased his coal at 6d. a load at the pit-head and subsequently retailed it to his parishioners for a shilling, thereby making a handsome profit of 100%.

Poet William Billington, after being compelled by ill-health to leave the factory, was for some time mine host of the Nag's Head. Here, in spite of sickness and domestic trouble, he wrote many of his finest lyrics and ballads.

George Hull, who was a distant relative, once said of Billington; "I shou'd think he was the most conscientious landlord I ever knew. He seemed always most firm in refusing to supply a drink to those who had already had as much as was good for them. After more than forty years I still think with the deepest gratitude and not without emotion, of his wise literary counsel and constant kindness."

Billington was not a facile writer and most of his work was written slowly and painfully, with many corrections and revisions. In 1883 he was persuaded to write a weekly series of local tales and sketches for the *Blackburn Standard* and a friend has recorded how laboriously the contributions were produced.

"Its more than flesh and blood can stand," mourned the poet, pointing to his almost illegible manuscript. "They want a whole column every week and its killing me, that's certain."

The name of the Joiner's Arms was changed to the Paganini when that eccentric musician chose this humble beerhouse for his lodging on the occasion of his only appearance in Blackburn. It was rumoured that when the unfortunate musician retired to his bedroom for the night, he found his couch already occupied by a noxious species of vermin only too common in that insalubrious locality, The result was that he spent the greater part of the night padding to and fro along Northgate in his carpet slippers, praying for the dawn.

As may be judged by the name, the Cockcrofts in Northgate marks the site of the town's earliest cockpit, which was located up a narrow entry adjoining the Paganini, and I have seen an 18th century document in which there was a reference to "the cock-house in Northgate." It may actually have been in the rear of the old inn itself, for many of the pits of the cock-fighting fraternity were attached to an inn.

*St. John's Church about the middle of the last century. The wardens used to meet in the nearby St. John's Tavern*

CHAPTER 2

# St. John's Tavern

SO far as I am aware, St. John's Tavern, which formerly stood at the corner of Ainsworth Street and Union Street, although one of Blackburn's oldest inns, was never a coaching inn or even a posting-house. These last were designed so that any man of means, travelling "post-haste" in his own coach or chaise, could hire a fresh relay of horses or a postillion and thus continue his journey with a minimum of delay.

Like most 18th century hostelries, however, it possessed ample stabling accommodation, mainly to "bait" the horses of farmers or local gentry riding in to market or bringing produce to the fair. Being somewhat remote from the town's main highways, mine host was content to leave stage coaches and the like to his brethren at the Old Bull or the Bay Horse. The inn's proximity to St. John's Church, however, made it the scene of many public meetings of an important and official nature.

At the opening of last century the duties of churchwardens were far more important and onerous than they are today, one of their functions being to perambulate the parish during the hours of divine service, magisterially inspecting all the local ale-houses and recording the names of all whom they should find indulging in an illicit pint during that prohibited period. Such culprits would be duly presented at the magistrate's court and fined.

Nevertheless, even these great officials themselves were not immune from human frailties, for I have records of more than one vestry meeting subsequently adjourning to St. John's Tavern. Doubtless the wardens and select vestrymen, soberly clad in their velvet knee breeches and buckled shoes, were merely desirous of continuing their grave discussions on church policy, but can one doubt that it would be over a friendly pipe and a stiff glass of toddy ?

One of the earliest references I have to this fine old inn is in connection with the annual dinner of the Company of Archers, a convivial society which flourished as early as 1794. On September 3rd, 1800, with their president, Mr. E. Chippendale in the chair, "Mirth and good humour prevailed in the highest degree, many excellent songs were sung and abundance of loyal and constitutional toasts most heartily bumpered." This we may well believe, for at a similar function held in the hotel in King

Street during the same year, no fewer than thirty-one separate healths were drunk, beginning with the Royal Family and probably ending with the landlord's cat. How many guests were then under the table is anyone's guess.

And speaking of chairs, there was a curious incident a year later which sparked off an editorial homily about improving the township's lighting, when a sedan chair was stolen from outside the inn "while the chairmen were transacting a little business within", and later found hidden behind the church, after the bellman had cried its loss through the streets. Such sedan chairs were then much in vogue as a fashionable means of conveyance, being greatly in demand by ladies proceeding to a dance or an assembly. They were carried by poles in the hands of two men and in shape were not unlike a hansom cab without wheels.

Like the early years of the present century, the outset of last century was one of crisis, when men were hourly in expectation of a French invasion. As a result, men's minds were exercised with problems of home defence and many loyal associations were formed. One of these was held in St. John's Tavern in August, 1803, when mine host was Thomas Stanley. Its purpose was to determine "on the most proper method of raising a volunteer corps of infantry for the defence of our King and Country."

An echo of this meeting is to be found in a subsequent announcement in the *Blackburn Mail* dated January 11th, 1804, which requires all men ballotted for the Militia, who have been approved, sworn and enrolled, or have provided fit persons to be their substitutes since the 11th day of May, 1803, and can swear that they are not in possession of £500, to apply for a bounty of six guineas, to which they are entitled. They were to apply for orders for payment therof to a meeting of the Deputy-Lieutenants "which will be holden for that purpose at St. John's Tavern."

Four years later Stanley had been succeeded by James Eastham, during whose tenancy the house was sold by auction. It was then described as "an old-established and well-accustomed house, pleasantly situated in Union Street, near St. John's Church, Blackburn, with the brewhouse and other suitable offices and conveniences belonging thereto." Other landlords included Robert Clarkson in 1824 and John Smith in 1855.

How the tavern came to be known to its habitues as "The Gaping Goose" I cannot tell, but must assume that it has some reference to its ecclesiastical associations. A favourite device greatly used by medieval masons and wood carvers in early churches was entitled "The Pelican in Piety", depicting that devoted bird feeding its young with its own blood. This was subsequently used as an inn sign, hence the colloquial nickname. Whether St. John's Tavern formerly bore this sign is a moot point, for we have no records, but the inference is obvious.

One of Blackburn's best known poets, Richard Dugdale, who achieved fame as "The Bard of Ribblesdale" also had a somewhat dubious connection with the old tavern. I quote without comment an extract from the Blackburn Alfred newspaper of February 15th, 1837 :

"John Thompson summoned Richard Dugdale for assault. Thompson stated that he keeps the St. John's Tavern and has back premises, part of which he lets to Dugdale as an engraver's shop. He made a door for Dugdale to go into his shop and Dugdale promised to put a lock on it but did not do so, and consequently thieves got into the yard and stole various articles. On Tuesday he got a man to put a bar on this door and Dugdale said he would break it off. A scuffle ensued and he laid Dugdale on his back "as nice as could be." But when he got up he knocked him (Thompson) down three times and made a pretty figure of his face. He could have "hided" him if he had liked but he would rather serve him out another way. After some argument the case was dismissed."

"Dickie" Dugdale was a robust character who, according to Billington, won laurels in the prize ring during his army days. Thanks to his proficiency in that gentle art he was often called upon to keep the peace when the parish constable was not to be found. I have a record of him being called to the Mason's Arms in Northgate, where one Miles Pollett "fro' Stanley House" was wrecking the premises in a drunken frolic. On seeing the burly poet, however, with his coat carelessly slung over his herculean shoulders, Pollett decided that discretion was the better part of valour and offered "Dickie" his hand instead of his fist.

**TO BE LET, BY TICKET,**

***At the house of Mr. Henry Sharples, the sign of the Montague Arms, King-street, Blackburn, in the County of Lancaster, on Monday the 18th April, 1831, at Six o'clock in the Evening, subject to such conditions as will be then and there produced,***

**ALL that newly-built and well-accustomed Inn, or PUBLIC HOUSE, known by the sign of the MONTAGUE ARMS, before mentioned, situate in King-street and corner of Montague-street, on the branch road leading to Preston, with the Brew-house, Shed for Coaches, two Stables, for nine horses, excellent Cellaring, extensive back Yard, and other conveniences thereunto belonging, and now in the occupation of *Mr. Henry Sharples* aforesaid.**

**The Premises may be entered upon immediately.**

**For Particulars apply to the said Mr. HENRY SHARPLES, or to Mr. JOHN IBBOTSON, King-street, the Owner.**

*Peel Fold, Knuzden, the original home of the Peel family*

CHAPTER 3

# A Doorway of Destiny

IF a local historian was asked to point out the spot within the Borough of Blackburn most intimately associated with its development, he would not, as one might imagine, select the entrance to its Victorian town hall. Instead, he would point to the subject of this chapter, the door of its Georgian Assembly Room.

Certainly the latter, which served not only as the doorway leading to the old Sessions room but was also the main entrance to the Hotel in King Street, has priority in point of age, as well as interest. Since its erection in 1804, this fine building (now serving as a labour exchange) has been identified with every phase of life in Regency Blackburn. Indeed, it is not too much to say that, during this eventful period, every townsman of note passed beneath that ornate portal (formerly graced by a pillared portico) and every event of importance has been transacted within those walls. May it long survive to remind us of a gracious past.

It was on February 3rd, 1802, that the editor of the *Blackburn Mail* announced that ". . . a very liberal subscription is entered into by the ladies and gentlemen of this town, towards the erection of an Assembly Room, to be built upon a large scale and elegant architecture and to have the advantage of a tavern." Will modern architects favour posterity by taking note of the word "elegant"!

Nevertheless, it reveals a curious lack of imagination on the part of the originators that such a commodious establishment, containing among other amenities seven eating rooms, twenty-five bedrooms and stabling for twenty horses, never received a name. In an era famous for quaint and even fantastic inn-signs and in a township possessing such gems as Doctor Syntax; Mother Redcap; Who could ha' thowt it; Stop and Rest; Hole i'th'Wall; and Gaping Goose, its proprietors were content with "The Hotel." It was not until many years later that the prefix Royal was added.

Its first landlord was William Brown, but three years later he was succeeded by Michael Whitehead, an enterprising character who inaugurated a stage coach service between Burnley and Preston, although with doubtful success. However, by 1824 the Hotel had become established as one of the town's chief coaching inns, for in that year the Invincible stage coach left the inn-yard for Leeds every morning at ten, returning at two in the afternoon with passengers en route for Preston and Liverpool. In addition a slow market coach arrived from Preston every Wednesday morning.

These stage coaches were the only public vehicles available for upwards of three centuries. The earliest were little better than springless covered wagons, with tyres nine inches broad to enable them to cope with the tremendous ruts in the ill-kept roads. It was only in Georgian times that they developed into the rakish turn-outs made familiar to us by the numerous old prints that still survive, preserved with loving care in many a wayside inn as a link with their romantic past.

By comparison with time-tables from neighbouring towns, it is possible to obtain some idea of the speed to which such conveyances attained. The journey to Preston, Burnley or Bolton, all within a range of some twelve miles, was completed in an hour and a half by stage coach and two hours by market coach, this including one change of horses. Thus we find that the average speed of a fast "flyer" was eight miles an hour, no mean feat considering the state of local road surfaces.

For many years the "quality" foregathered at the Hotel for celebrations and rejoicings, adjourning to the attached Assembly Room in Heaton Street for dancing and musical entertainment. Here it is on record that in January, 1814, " . . . there was a grand Ball at our Assembly Room in honour of the late glorious victories by Lord Wellington and our brave allies . . . which was attended by the youth, beauty and fashion of the town. The room was magnificently decorated with laurel, &c."

But let us turn back the pages of history for some of its civic associations. Within four years of its erection we find a meeting of townsfolk in the Hotel for the purpose of sending a memorial to the Postmaster-General asking that the London Mail Coach might pass through Blackburn instead of through Chorley to expedite local deliveries, a request duly granted.

The turning of a leaf reveals a different scene, involving the impotent protest of handloom weavers against wartime privations and loss of trade, when " . . . the 48th Regiment of Foot arrived from Preston and paraded in the Hotel yard. Very soon after upwards of 1,500 people blocked up the entrances, breaking the windows, shouting and huzzaing in a hideous manner." They were finally dispersed and the ringleaders captured.

With the coming of peace, however, a new era of prosperity seemed to have dawned and the event was celebrated in no uncertain fashion. One distinctive feature of the rejoicings consisted of a series of transparencies erected along all the main thoroughfares. Over the doorway of the Hotel mine host hung a scene illuminated from within depicting Bonaparte climbing a ladder with rungs labelled "Spain, Prussia," &c. and John Bull in the act of tumbling him down.

We turn over another page to find ourselves involved in a religious dispute, when a poll of ley-payers was held in the Sessions room to decide upon the levying of a church rate for lighting and heating the newly-erected parish church in September, 1827, when " . . . a considerable number of the canaille surrounded the outer door the whole day and it was with difficulty that any person of respectability could approach it."

But the brightest page of its history was written during the year of the township's Incorporation, for it was in the Sessions room that the original petition to the Queen for a Charter was drawn up under the auspices of William Hoole on November 28th, 1850. And it was here, some twelve months later, that the first meeting of the new Town Council was held to elect J. W. Hornby as their Charter Mayor, together with the town clerk and other officials.

In an article of this nature one can do little more than brush the fringe of the many momentous happenings associated with this fine old building but maybe I have said enough to emphasise their importance. Steeped as it is in tradition, it must always hold a cherished place in the affection of all true Blackburnians.

---

*Bygone Penny Street. The Waterloo Inn can be seen just behind the haycart*

CHAPTER 4

# Bygone Penny Street

STUDENTS of local history are apt to regard Blackburn's Incorporation in 1851 as the starting point of all the town's administrative improvements. Yet for many years prior to this date it was governed by a conscientious body of Improvement Commissioners, who not only laid down the lines of the existing town centre, erected the old Market House and effected countless street improvements, but also kept an eye on the housing situation.

From some of their reports it would appear that Penny Street was one of the town's black spots. Here, in 1842, " . . . there were many houses without any troughs whatever, whilst in other cases the spouts from the roofs did not reach within three or four feet from the ground. Under these spouts it was customary in rainy weather to place tubs and mugs, which could not but be a great nuisance on the footpath."

Possibly for this reason, although its line lay along the ancient highway into Yorkshire, it was never regarded as a desirable residential area. Indeed, for long enough, it was looked upon as the town's Irish quarter and as such, to be patrolled by policemen in couples and regarded askance by Tory politicians. In 1868, for instance, it was the scene of a lively election skirmish, which was only broken up when the redoubtable "Jackie" Smith, Blackburn's rough-hewn mayor, threatened to call out the military and have the contestants "shot like rapputs."

Penny Street gets its curious name from the fact that when the glebe land was opened-up hereabouts in 1796 for building purposes, the ground was let at a rent charge of 1d. per square yard. By 1822 it boasted no fewer than seven inns or taverns. These included the Mason's Arms, the Doctor Syntax, the Golden Fleece, the Plough, the Waterloo Inn, the rounded corner of which can just be seen over the hay cart on the left of our illustration, at the junction of Larkhall Street, the Lord Nelson and, last but not least, the Bay Horse.

Owing to the lack of a suitable lock-up, it was the custom at this time to make use of the cellars of various local inns as a place of confinement for prisoners awaiting trial. Among these were both the Britannia and the Fleece in Penny Street. In 1805 John Hall was mine host of the Golden Fleece and he even went so far as to draw up a scale of charges for such unwilling guests. Here is the preamble to his notice in the *Blackburn Mail.*

"To Constables, Manufacturers, &c. Whereas it frequently happens that vagabonds, depredators and thieves of various descriptions, after being taken into custody, are . . . obliged to wait some time in Blackburn, John Hall, publican, in Penny Street, hereby gives notice that he has a safe and commodious lock-up house on his premises, and will be answerable for, and will properly secure, any vagabond, &c. placed under his care . . . at the rate of 1s. per day and 1s. 6d. per night."

The Lord Nelson, which finally disappeared together with the Bay Horse to make room for our new market, had some pretensions to dignity and in 1807 was a coaching house, and is of interest as being one of Blackburn's first connecting links with the rising holiday resort of Blackpool.

The announcement reads: "Preston, Lytham and Blackpool coach. Cheap and expeditious travelling from Mr. Sharpe's, the Lord Nelson Inn, Blackburn, in a commodious coach called the Trafalgar, every Sunday and Wednesday mornings at 7 o'clock precisely. Reaches the Dog Inn, Preston, at half-past nine and arrives at Blackpool at four in the evening . . . "

In the same year the inn obtained rather more doubtful notoriety when it became the scene of an exploit by a certain "son of Crispin," who, the editor of the *Mail* observes, "devoured four pounds and a half of bacon, fried, together with forty eggs. We know not what weight of bread he consumed at the time, but after finishing the bacon and eggs, he mixed to the fat remaining, wherein they were fried, a quantity of vinegar, sopped bread therein, devouring the same also, leaving no remainder whatsoever."

But the Bay Horse was undoubtedly one of the town's oldest coaching inns. Although not marked on Lang's map of 1739, it figured largely in local annals before the close of the 18th century. At that time Salford terminated at the old hump-back bridge in a veritable bottle-neck, the Bay Horse projecting so far across the highway as to narrow the approach to less than twenty feet.

When the ancient bridge was first widened in 1846, the Bay Horse Inn, together with the adjoining Lord Nelson, were both demolished, set back some fifty feet and re-built in the substantial Victorian style they retained to the end. As we may see from Charles Haworth's well-known drawing, the original Bay Horse was a square-fronted structure of late Queen Anne style, with ugly proportions and roof of grey slate. The courtyard, where the sweating coach teams and post horses were groomed and baited, was approached from Water Street, adjoining the site of the *Blackburn Mail* office. Until the recent demolitions several old cottages stood in this vicinity and must often have witnessed the start of the long coach journey to Manchester.

The earliest notice of the inn's coaching activities is dated September 4th, 1793, when we learn that the Manchester Accommodation Coach began to run from Mr. Pickup's the Bay Horse, Salford, on Mondays, Wednesdays and Fridays, leaving at one o'clock and arriving at the Star Inn, Deansgate, at six. From this we may see that the distance was covered in five hours, averaging little more than five miles an hour. Yet even this snail's pace, owing to the appalling state of the Bolton turnpike, was not achieved without tremendous exertions on the part of the wretched horses. Later this rate was considerably accelerated, for in 1825 the Wellington and Commercial coaches frequently covered this distance of twenty-four miles in the space of two hours and forty minutes, including stoppages.

Probably the most remarkable incident in the history of this fine old inn occurred when it was captured by rioters during the loom-breaking riots of 1826 and used as their headquarters. Taking possession of cellar and larder, they compelled the widowed tenant, Mary Rigby, to wait upon their needs until her stocks were exhausted.

Salford Bridge was the only strategic point of any value to the forces of law and order against a mob coming into town from the direction of Accrington. Had this crossing been held by a single troop of the 1st Dragoon Guards, who then garrisoned the town, it is probable that the scenes of devastation at the old Dandy Factory and other neighbouring mills would never have occurred. Instead the cavalry advanced and actually rode through the advancing mob of armed weavers near Furthergate, under the impression that the real centre of the outbreak was still at Sykes' mill in Accrington.

*Blakeley Moor with the Golden Ball on the left and the Sawley Arms in the centre*

CHAPTER 5

# Old Blakeley Moor

MY earliest recollections of old-time Blakeley Moor date back to those remote days at the beginning of this century when as a schoolboy I skirted its insalubrious purlieus on my unwilling way to the old Public Higher Grade School at the top of Montague Street. Having express orders to pass it by with averted eyes, its unhallowed ginnels and alleyways always had a dreadful fascination for me and I fear I witnessed more than one drunken brawl in the vicinity of the Golden Ball Inn, now happily swept away into the rubbish heap of the past. But that, of course, was in its years of decline; in earlier times it had a far higher standing.

In 1891, when its abolition was first mooted, Blakeley Moor was described as " . . . the mass of poor and squalid property with which the Technical School is surrounded. A triangular-shaped area of mean-looking tenements, including within it the salubrious localities of Cannon Street and Engine Street. A good proportion of the property is in a dilapidated condition, it abounds in tramps' lodgings and houses of an even worse description."

Yet the Moor had seen better days and some of its houses were originally erected as the mansions of local cotton manufacturers. Most of the property dated back to the reign of George III, when the area, a large tract of common land on which cattle grazed and geese cackled, was first developed for building purposes. Hence Queen Street was named after Queen Charlotte, Duke Street after the Duke of Kent and the Cock-crofts after the old cock-pit standing in the vicinity. Engine Street was so-called because it housed Blackburn's first manual fire engine and Cannon Street because its Northgate end was blocked to wheeled traffic by an old Crimean cannon which protruded from the pavement by way of a stoop.

In his reminiscences of old Blackburn Tom Dobson once wrote: "The old Golden Ball played a prominent part in many exciting scenes on the Moor for a hundred years or more. The first landlord I know was named Lawson. He died about 1836. The next was Thomas Roberts, who served his time as a painter with Thomas Boardman of Fleming Square. I remember the hustings erected in front of the house at the 1835 election and the crowd of gaily-decorated people on the Moor, wearing green and white for Bowring, red and purple for Turner and blue and white for Feilden. The Golden Ball and the old Cross Keys were the chief resorts of farmers and cattle jobbers who attended the cattle and pig markets."

This old inn was also for many years the headquarters of visiting showmen, such as the Wild family, who erected their booths and roundabouts on the Moor in time for the Easter Fair. Wild's Show was one of the great attractions, with its clowns and mountebanks. Dobson recalls that one year a French acrobat attached to the show sat on the roof slates of the Golden Ball, which was three storeys high, whilst he affixed a gigantic pair of stilts to his legs, on which he subsequently paraded nonchalantly along Northgate and across the Moor to an adjacent woodyard. Sam and Tom Wild lived to a great age, both dying in 1884 within a few days of each other in the caravan where they had spent most of their working lives.

Other attractions to these early Easter fairs were Pablo's Circus, Swallow's mountebanks, Sam Well's Circus and Wombwell's Menagerie. Stalls were erected in various places for the sale of ginger bread, Eccles cakes, nuts, brandysnaps and other delicacies beloved of children. To accommodate their elders, local publicans could obtain a three-day licence for the sale or ale and spirits, hiring houses in the vicinity or setting up wooden booths.

Although these were the days before steam or electric traction had been evolved, there were still a goodly number of roundabouts. These were propelled by a number of hired youths concealed within. They pushed at a long wooden bar, and were allowed to take an occasional ride themselves by way of payment for their services.

Needless to say, the Golden Ball did a roaring trade on such occasions. It is also remembered for an incident during one of Mrs. Lewis's Teetotal crusades. George Graham, an old soldier, was her mission door-keeper. Although a reformed character, he had his moments of weakness and when, one day, he failed to report for duty, she feared the worst.

At once she was on his track, searching every inn and tavern in the vicinity until ultimately her lost sheep was found, maudlin and very much the worse for wear, in the Golden Ball. Undaunted, she entered the forbidden portals and brought him away in triumph, under the very nose of the astounded inn-keeper. She then escorted him home, saw him safely put to bed and then sat up with his wife until closing time. Next morning she was back again at 5 a.m. to make sure he went to work at Yates and Thom's Foundry.

Our illustration is a drawing of old Cannon Street, and the Golden Ball is the tall, dark building on the left-hand side of the street. It stood at the corner, with its front facing the Technical School.

One of the half-dozen oldest taverns in Blackburn was undoubtedly the Cross Keys, which stood at the north-west end of the Moor. This sign was originally taken from the arms of the Papal See but was frequently used after the Reformation as it also embodied the arms of several Bishoprics. The old inn was known to Peter Walkden, the Dissenting

Minister. Here, according to his diary, he met a friend on September 9th, 1729, and drank a pot of cider. Towards the end of that century it was tenanted by Henry Stanley, who died in 1804. The premises were then advertised for sale, as a " . . . public-house situate on Blakeley Moor, called the Cross Keys, with brewhouse, &c., occupied by Mr. Thomas Bannister, with the dwelling-house adjoining, two cottages, a smithy, joiner's shop, &c."

In 1822 it was occupied by William Bramley, who married Mary, the daughter of Henry Stanley, and two years later another sister, Margaret, appears to have succeeded, for old Peggy Stanley of the Cross Keys became a character remembered locally by many residents long after she had passed away.

Other inns on the Moor included the Freemason's Tavern, the Roebuck Inn, St. Paul's Tavern and the Globe Inn. This last was described in 1809 as " . . . all that large, commodious and well-accustomed inn, commonly known by the name of the Globe, with brewhouse and other conveniences and appurtenancies belonging thereto, now in the possession of John Parker."

*The House of Correction which stood on the old Darwen Street bridge*

CHAPTER 6

# Old-Time Darwen Street

AN early-Victorian reveller who chose Darwen Street for the scene of his operations would have found plenty of scope. According to Baines' Gazetteer of 1824 there were no fewer than a round dozen inns, most of which survived into the Victorian era. He would undoubtedly have commenced at the Old Bull, which, although its front door was in Church Street, had a side-entry into the courtyard from Darwen Street.

Then, with a cautious glance at the house and butcher's shop next door, tenanted by none other than burly John Kay, Blackburn's highly efficient deputy constable, he would have looked in at the Legs of Man, four doors lower down.

The history of this fine old inn reaches back into the Middle Ages. According to some historians, it was formerly known as the Paslew's Arms and under the auspices of the abbots of Whalley, including the ill-fated John Paslew, was the resort of pilgrims as early as the 14th century.

Paslew, who was executed at Lancaster for the part he took in the futile "Pilgrimage of Grace" in 1537, was closely connected with Blackburn, having re-edified the ancient market cross, which stood at the junction of Darwen Street and Church Street. From this spot on market days the stalls of local farmers, hucksters and itinerant traders stretched almost as far as Mill Lane. They had a prescriptive right to use the footpath for this purpose, a right which I believe still appertains to shop-keepers in the vicinity and still emphasised by the double width of the flagged causeway.

The old inn was in close proximity both to Hallows Spring, which in medieval times was famous for its healing properties and as such the object of many pious pilgrimages. Doubtless the inn was retained as a rest-house by the monks of Whalley after their translation from Stanlaw. The gift of the living of the parish church was vested in the abbots of that great Cistercian abbey, the vicar being usually one of the brethren, so that pilgrimages to the holy well and the shrine of St. Mary would be sure of every encouragement.

Of the mixed company thus entertained, gallant knights and their ladies, church dignitaries, substantial merchants and their dames, pert esquires, palmers and the like, one would need the genius of a Chaucer to do full justice, but that such colourful guests were entertained within a stones-throw of Blackburn market cross, there is no shadow of a doubt.

In later years the inn lost something of its original status. The sign of the Legs of Man was probably adopted at the time of the Reformation, as this device is the cognisance of the Earls of Derby as lords of the Isle of Man, and we know that Thomas, 2nd Earl of Derby founded a chantry in the ancient parish church some years before that event. It was subsequently dissolved but the family retained their influence in the town for many years after. We have no record of the inn's original appearance but it would be substantially similar to the neighbouring Old Bull, which was a timber-framed structure with overhanging gables facing the street. The existing fabric appears to be late Georgian, with no distinctive architectural features. Connected with the hostelry, however, are a series of massive vaults extending under the highway, which are still regarded as excellent examples of late barrel-vaulting.

The inn was never used as a posting-house, but for many years during the holiday season a special coach set out from its stable-yard for the benefit of local gentry, merchants and manufacturers travelling to Lytham and Blackpool for rest and recuperation. It was started by W. Frankland in 1833, leaving every Thursday and Saturday morning at 6.30.

At that time Blackpool consisted merely of a couple of small hotels and a few cottages for the accommodation of boarders and among the attractions offered to visitors was a newsroom and circulating library, a ride on horseback or in a carriage along the sands and a company of comedians whose auditorium was in a barn. It is amusing to recall the stringent regulations governing sea-bathing. Propriety was de rigueur.

"The time of bathing is generally at the flood when, the company being driven from the shore, the place is more private. A bell rings at the time of bathing, as a signal for the ladies. Some use machines drawn by one horse, a few travel from their apartments in their water-dress but the majority unclothe in the boxes which stand on the beach for their use. If a gentleman is seen on the parade, he forfeits a bottle of wine. When the ladies retire, the bell rings for the gentlemen, who act a second part in the same scene."

Three doors lower down was the Bird-in-Hand Inn, better known to a later generation as the County Arms, the records of which go back to 1794. There was quite a cluster of these old-fashioned inns at the top of Darwen Street in those early days. They were necessary to accommodate the throngs of country folk attending the market with carts and pack animals to dispose of their produce by sale or barter.

John Wood was mine host of the Bird-in-Hand in 1794 and from Baines' Gazetteer we learn that John Haworth ruled its destiny in 1824. At that time the Bury and Haslingden carriers baited at this depot, the Bury wagon setting out on Wednesday after the market closed, travelling all night and returning on Friday morning.

Some time after 1832 Wood was succeeded by Henry Whalley, who established a coaching service between Blackburn and Bolton, driving the four-in-hand himself. A rival coach, operated by Bland, started from the Eagle and Child opposite and as both were timed to leave at the same hour, the journey often developed into a neck-and-neck race not always appreciated by nervous passengers, who doubtless had vivid recollections of serious accidents arising from such contests of skill and nerve. Whalley drove harder but Bland was reputed to be the better driver.

When the railway reached Blackburn from Bolton in August, 1847, it marked the end of the coaching era. The Sough tunnel was the last part of the work to be completed and whilst boring operations were still in progress, the railway company had vehicles waiting to convey passengers by road between trains waiting at each end of the tunnel. Whalley's coach was among the very last to give up the unequal struggle but in the same issue of the *Blackburn Standard* which announced the running of trains through the tunnel appeared a notice dated October 13th, 1847. It ran as follows:

"To coach and omnibus proprietors, innkeepers, postmasters, farmers, &c. To be sold by auction at the Bird-in-Hand Inn, the whole of the coaching establishment of Mr. Henry Whalley, consisting of 30 good-bred and well-seasoned horses, 5 coaches, 1 omnibus and 6 four-horse sets of capital harness, the whole in good working order, he having discontinued working them in consequence of the railway being partly opened to Bolton."

Thus, like many a similar struggle being waged throughout the country, the old order reluctantly made way for the new.

**SNIG BROOK BREWERY,**
**BLACKBURN.**
**JAMES CUNNINGHAM'S**
**BITTER & PALE ALES, PORTER, &c.**
FOR HOME CONSUMPTION, AT HIS BREWERY,
**6 PEEL STREET, BLACKBURN.**

*Orders Addressed to SPRING BURN HOUSE, MONTAGUE STREET, or the BREWERY, will receive immediate attention.*

*The Queen's Head on the left, associated with the riots of 1826 and 1842*

CHAPTER 7

# The Loom-breaking Riots

ONE of the best-known and most characteristic of Charles Haworth's drawings of old Blackburn is his view of Darwen Street in the vicinity of Dandy Walk. It was made at the suggestion of William Hulme, who was a compositor on the staff of the *Blackburn Times* and contributed the folklore sections to J. C. Shaw's "Bits of Old Blackburn." He drew the artist's attention to this little cluster of ancient tenements, so near the town centre, as one of the most picturesque and in imminent danger of early demolition.

He was mistaken, for by some curious chance, with the exception of the Old Bull Hotel, all the property north of Dandy Walk has survived and retains much of its old-world aspect, in spite of the paint and stucco of repeated renovations. This applies particularly to the old Queen's Head Inn, the house on the left of our illustration and the dwelling-house adjoining, which is not shown.

This latter was at one time the home of Joseph Harrison, the Ingleton blacksmith who left his smithy in Dandy Walk to build Bank Foundry and thereby lay the foundations of the town's engineering trade. This humble dwelling was the birthplace of his son Henry the philanthropist, to whom we owe the Harrison Gymnasium and Institute.

But Charles Haworth had other, and more personal associations with this area, for it was here, as a young man of 26, that he witnessed the attack on the Dandy Factory by plug-drawing rioters in 1842. At the time his father had a drapery business on a site where the Old Bank now stands, and having received timely warning, he and his son hastily shuttered the shop windows and hurried the rest of the family upstairs out of harm's way.

But one of the upper windows looked out across the old Market Place and through a crack in the casement the venturesome Charles witnessed Montague Feilden reading the Riot Act and saw a contingent of the 72nd Highlanders, after firing a warning volley over the heads of the mob, lower their pieces and take aim at the ring-leaders.

He recalled that the shutters of the Eagle and Child Inn were completely riddled and that a well-known character named Harry King only saved his skin by wedging himself as stiff as a poker in the archway leading to the courtyard of the Old Bull.

The old Queen's Head was in the very vortex of this maelstrom of disorder, as it had been during the earlier loom-breaking riots of 1826. On the later occasion a number of prisoners were held by the military in the Queen's Head and it was a determined effort to rescue them on the part of the rioters that led to the ensuing bloodshed. The incident is described in the *Blackburn Standard* of August 17th, 1842:

"The numbers of the crowd were frightfully increased and there was every appearance of a general attack by some thousands on the military, for the purpose of rescuing the prisoners. However, an additional force of the 72nd Highlanders marched down to Mr. Eccles' Mill, where the prisoners were secured, and shortly Mr. Blomley of the Bull Inn drove down a coach-and-four for the purpose of removing the prisoners to the barrack-yard. On arrival at the lane leading to the mill, the horses were stopped by the crowd but on some soldiers coming forward the rioters gave way and Mr. Blomley with a good whip-hand turned his team neatly round and backed in the coach towards the mill.

"The coach was then filled with prisoners, some of them thus enjoying the comforts of an inside seat and being strongly guarded with a strong force of military with fixed bayonets, moved up Darwen Street. It had not, however, advanced far from the entrance to the mill when a rush of the mob was made and a shower of stones let fly at the military. The order to fire was immediately given and the rear-guard fired."

It was easy for a mob of rioters to provide themselves with ammunition in those days, for Darwen Street was paved with small cobble-stones, which could be prized up from the ground with a jemmy or even the blade of a strong knife. King Street was also paved with these rounded cobbles, which were merely water-worn stones collected from the sea shore or the bed of a river, and when the Hornby residence was attacked in 1841 it is on record that over a ton of such stones were flung through the windows.

In happier days the old Queen's Head (which formerly bore a painted sign over its door depicting the bust of good Queen Anne), was the favourite place of call for the quieter type of market clientele. Here demure housewives in poke bonnets and hooped petticoats, clinging to the arms of stout, bewhiskered burghers in embroidered waistcoats and buckled shoes, called for a modest pot of cider or a glass of wine, to alleviate the thirst acquired by forcing their way through a confused arrary of carts and pack-horses, farmer's wains and webster's "galls", loaded with whisket and pannier.

Meanwhile, serenely aloof from the bustle, yet benignly conscious of his authority, the town constable, honest Tom Greenall, George Clayton or in later years John Kay, would survey the colourful scene, idly swinging his painted staff and touching his beaver hat to the local gentry.

The corner of Dandy Walk opposite the Queen's Head was occupied by John Myer, saddler, as seen in our drawing and next door was the premises of John Polding, miller, who at one time owned and operated Blackburn's only windmill on the canal bank at Eanam. As a child I remember surveying its ancient foundations and wondering if it had been the site of some bygone circus. The two shops in question remained until the erection of the General Post Office and their projecting gables are obviously Jacobean.

A little further along, at the corner of a cul-de-sac later opened up as Jubilee Street, was the old White Bull Inn. Little is known of this quaint old hostelry but I have a note that at one time it had a large room reserved for the sitting of an impromptu magistrate's court. It was conveniently close to the former town lock-up or House of Correction, which stood on the south side of Darwen Street Bridge. In 1663 it was known as "The Dungeon" and the prison proper was a damp rat-infested vault below ground level and liable to flooding, being adjacent to the river. To add to the prisoner's worries, the adjoining cellar was used as a powder magazine, so that he was threatened with the peril of both fire and water.

Whilst George Clayton (who gave his name to Clayton Street) was constable in 1800, two men escaped from this lock-up. The first of these local Jack Sheppards was an agitator named Robinson, who subsequently lost his wig and almost his life, at Peterloo. Some of his fellow reformers filled the lock of the door with gunpowder abstracted from the magazine and touched it off with a match.

The second escape was even more bizarre. This time the prisoner removed the iron bars from his cell window, which overlooked the river, He gave himself up the next day, paid a small fine and on returning to his employment at Threlfall's blacksmith shop, was given the job of replacing the prison bars and making them secure against further prison breaks.

*Queen Street, Blakeley Moor in 1904, looking towards Northgate and the entrance to Town Hall Street*

CHAPTER 8

# The Town's Moor

THAT "well-accustomed" inn, bearing for its sign the name of the Duke of York, is one of the few remaining hostelries in Blackburn to retain something of its original features. The royal duke from whom it took its name was the son of George III and held the office of commander-in-chief of the British Army until his death in 1827. His memory is still kept green by many an old country tavern in the north of England.

The inn itself was established about 1790 and its formal brick facade fronting upon Darwen Street is typical of that period. The rear of the premises is possibly earlier being built of well-cut blocks of freestone. Part of it was formerly used as a shoeing forge and the well-worn stone mounting block, for the use of farmers' wives riding pillion, is still in position.

The inn's isolated position on the edge of the town's moor must have made it a welcome sight to travellers descending the lonely, highwayman-infested moorland roads from Haslingden and Bolton and many a weary horseman must have halted here for a stirrup cup to celebrate his safe arrival. That the Bolton and Manchester turnpike swarmed with footpads may be judged from the fact that it was the custom for local manufacturers and merchants to redezvous at the edge of the town hereabouts and travel over the moors under the protection of an armed escort. There can be little doubt that the Duke of York inn was one such meeting place.

The town moor, reserved by decree for the training of military levies since the days of the first Elizabeth, was constantly in use during the critical days of the Napoleonic wars. Indeed, the town's powder magazine, after its transfer from the old lock-up cellar, stood at the junction of Park Road and Bolton Street, and the near proximity of so many thirsty militia-men, after performing their varied evolutions under the stern eye of a red-sashed drill sergeant, must have resulted in many a profitable raid on mine host's ale-barrels.

It is recorded that, during the premature peace celebrations of 1814, the licensee, one Thomas Holden, displayed no fewer than three trans-parencies, these being appropriate devices painted on oiled silk and illuminated from behind by lamps or candles. The first of these was a portrait of the Prince Regent, supported by justice and peace; the second was Lord Wellington, supported by Britannia and the third a Cossack in full gallop, all with suitable mottoes.

Christopher Gibson succeeded Holden and during his time the inn was the scene of a lively episode arising out of the loom-breaking riots of 1826.

On April 18 one of the Manchester market coaches was attacked by a mob in Blackburn old market place, resulting in some bloodshed. One of the ring-leaders, a weaver named Thomas Bury, was taken prisoner and confined in the cellar of the Duke of York. Undismayed, however, the rioters waited till the soldiers had returned to barracks, then battered down the front door and effected his rescue.

But John Kay, Blackburn's efficient constable, was not a man to be thus deflected from the path of duty. In the early hours of next morning, when the excitement had subsided, he coolly forced his way into Bury's home and again arrested him, this time in bed.

From the Duke of York Inn, retracing our steps towards the town centre, we next come to the Hare and Hounds and the Ship Inn. The latter stood on the west side of the street where it began to rise to surmount the ancient stone bridge over the Blakewater. Somewhat set back from the street line, it existed as long ago as 1784 and only disappeared when the improvement was affected which opened up Mincing Lane into Darwen Street.

In 1824 the landlord of the Three Crowns Inn was Edmund Holden. The premises were on the north side of Mill Lane and have a sinister association, for it was here that James Barker, (who resided next door), was arrested in 1803 for the forgery of a Bank of England note. The unfortunate man was tried at Lancaster Assizes and hanged, his body being subsequently brought back to Blackburn and buried in the parish church yard. He was regarded as the victim of a cruel and unjust sentence and the funeral was made the occasion of a procession of sympathisers.

Two doors nearer the town centre stood the old Anchor Inn, a building of Jacobean origin. Demolished about 1870, it was originally the town house of one of the lesser gentry. In its later days the windows facing the street were guarded by heavy shutters, obviously indicating that mine host, having suffered from the effects of two pitched battles between loom-breaking rioters and the military almost on his doorstep in 1826 and 1842, was taking no more chances of stray bullets or cobble stones.

At the close of the 18th century the situation of the Anchor Inn was undoubtedly in Darwen Street but according to a notice dating back to about 1750 it would appear to have been located in Church Street. This reads as follows : "To be sold by auction at the sign of the Black Bull, a large house now occupied by Mr. John Tattersall, known by the sign of the Anchor in Church Street, Blackburn, with a stable, smithy and garden adjoining, the whole held by lease under the Rector of Blackburn."

There is a simple explanation for this anomaly. In the 18th century there was some considerable latitude in the actual nomenclature of our main streets. Thus, in a sales bill dated 18th February, 1799, the White Bull Inn is described as situated in Darwen Street, otherwise Church Street.

King Street provides another such instance, for in many early deeds it is designated Sudell Street, alias King Street.

Continuing northward from the Anchor towards the market cross we find in the old tenements adjoining Margaret Brown, confectioner; Richard Robinson, saddler and William Preston, butcher. Then came the Wheatsheaf Inn (mine host Henry Whittaker), which was subsequently demolished and re-built on its present site in Mincing Lane to open up the way into St. Peter Street.

The Eagle and Child Inn, our last port of call, was old-established in 1790 and belonged to the same owner as the Wheatsheaf. In 1803 both were sold together ". . . at the house of James Walmsley, the Wheatsheaf in Blackburn, with the warehouse, brewhouse, stable, &c. belonging thereto and now occupied by Mrs. Hannah Haydock. Also a messuage or dwelling-house and butcher's shop adjoining, with the rooms over the gateway leading into Market Street Lane; also the beneficial interest of Miss Thornber and other in the leasehold messuage or public-house, commonly called the Eagle and Child."

In April, 1821, the *Blackburn Mail* reports an accident to Ralph Booth, of the Eagle and Child Inn, who, "returning home in a gig, the vehicle upset while turning into Northgate, and Mr. Booth had his thigh broken." In his time, during the loom-breaking riots, the shutters of the old inn were riddled with bullets and one man was severely wounded whilst sheltering in the doorway.

*Bank House from the grounds of which Blackburn was bombarded in 1642*

CHAPTER 9

# The Golden Lion

BEFORE Victoria Street was first laid out, the short length or road between Lord Street and the bottom of Church Street was actually part of Ainsworth Street, which wound round between the old property in Lower Church Street and the Theatre Royal. At the junction there was a dangerous bottle-neck formed by the protruding gable of the Feilden manorhouse, which then stood on the site of the Penny Bank.

The street hereabouts was too narrow to allow two carts to pass abreast, but having passed this hazard, the driver of the eastward-bound vehicle would emerge on to a wide open area almost treble the normal street width. There is a good reason for this. In the 16th century Salford Bridge was only a bridle bridge, too narrow for the passage of wheeled traffic and in consequence the road forked at this point, one branch leading to the bridge and the other to a ford a little way upstream, from which one emerged at the bottom of Water Street, almost facing the old Bay Horse Inn.

This approach was dominated by another ancient hostelry, the Golden Lion, which, having survived the perils of fire and flood for some three centuries, was swept away by the hand of man a few years ago.

I have no record as to when this fine old inn first became a coaching house. It is not mentioned as such by Baines in 1824, when its landlord was Joseph Duxbury, and its address 24 Church Street. Then, it must be remembered, the numbering of houses was consecutive, and 1, Church Street, the shop of William Earl, tailor, was on the north side of Higher Church Street, for King William Street had not come into existence. Immediately to the east of the Golden Lion was the shop of J. W. Astley, bookseller and binder, followed by that of John Martin, stay-maker; John McKean, brazier; Susannah Brown, milliner; William Aspinall, attorney and finally the residence of Thomas Dugdale, surgeon. This last was a handsome Georgian mansion standing at the corner now occupied by Woolworth's stores.

Prior to 1825 Blackburn's four coaching inns appear to have been the Old Bull, the Hotel in King Street, the Bay Horse and the New Inn. On November 30th of that year, however, a notice, embellished by a vigorous woodcut of a stage coach in full career, appeared on the front of the *Blackburn Mail*, informing all and sundry that the elegant "Royal Union" coach would leave Mr. Duxbury's Golden Lion Inn Church Street every Tuesday and Friday morning at 4.30 (for the accommodation of corn merchants) and on Monday, Wednesday, Thursday and Saturday morning at 6.45 for Liverpool, returning the same day, all at reduced prices.

From this emphasis on reduced prices, it would seem that mine host had established a "pirate" coach in an endeavour to capture the regular trade. This was a common cause of friction and often led to breakneck races between rivals along the narrow cobbled streets. When competition was keen and passengers scarce, rather than proceed with empty seats on their vehicles, proprietors would take passengers free of charge and if need be, stand them a drink as an added inducement.

Whether the attempt in this case succeeded we have no means of knowing, but it can be said that for many years the Golden Lion yard was a depot for stage wagons, or land carriers, as they were termed. In 1824 Thomas Ellis left at 8 a.m. on Wednesdays and Saturdays for Colne and Burnley, whilst John and James Radcliffe left for Haslingden on Saturdays at the same time. Behind the inn was a large courtyard with ample stable accommodation, so good, indeed, that until recent times it was in use as a livery stable.

Here, John Haydock, cab proprietor, had his office. John was a most original character and his reminiscences were as varied as they were piquant. One of his favourite yarns concerned a corpulent town councillor who entered his first cab in a terrific hurry to get to an important meeting at the town hall. Unfortunately, his excessive bulk was too much for the cab bottom, which fell through, there-by compelling its occupant, much against his will, to run the whole way. His remarks at the end of this uncomfortable journey have not come down to posterity.

Several of the licensees of the Golden Lion were also well-known local characters. In 1852 Thomas Kenyon controlled its destiny, whilst some years later he was succeeded by Robert Riding, better known to his generation as "Cock Robin", a noted sportsman, who died in 1857.

For generations the Golden Lion was famous for its excellent "home-brewed" and its cellars were stocked with many a hogshead of the best. But there were occasions when they overflowed with another liquid of a less desirable nature. Because of its low-lying situation, the inn was subject to extensive flooding whenever the River Blakewater was in turbulent mood. In 1729 twelve persons were drowned in the vicinity by a sudden inundation, while the year 1792 was long spoken of as that of the great flood, when hundreds of houses in the town centre were waterlogged and four residents lost their lives.

I have vivid recollections of the flood of November 12, 1901, when a depth of 3 feet 6 inches was recorded in Water Street, for once appropriately named. On this occasion the cellars of the Golden Lion were completely submerged and mine host, Mr. Alec Forbes had the doubtful pleasure of seeing his beer barrels floating leisurely towards the bottom of Church Street, in company with sundry apple tubs, orange boxes and other flotsam of a dubious nature.

In this age of television and cinema we are sometimes apt to forget that such old inns as the Golden Lion were an integral part of the town's social life. Here our fathers gathered to hear the latest news, to await the arrival of the stage coach, to discuss urgent political issues and to whisper current scandal. In the light of our modern problems and their sociological implications, we are beginning to realise that where these early days were perhaps lacking in breadth of outlook, they were made up in great part by a wealth of local intimacy and good neighbourliness, virtues we are rapidly losing today.

GOLDEN ♦ LION ♦ HOTEL,

CHURCH STREET, BLACKBURN.

*One Minute's Walk from the Railway Station.*

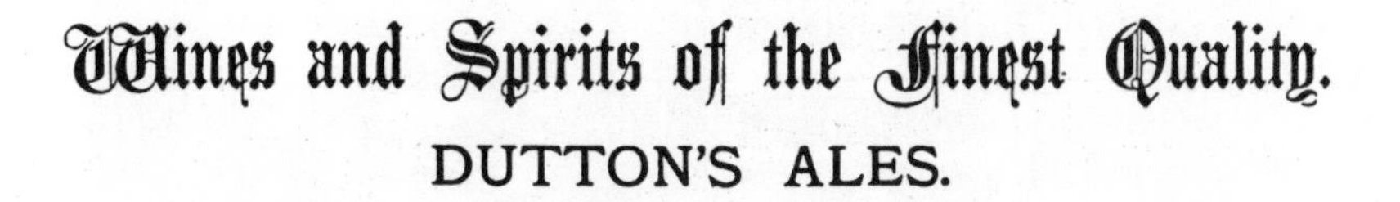


DUTTON'S ALES.

Head-quarters of the Blackburn and District Canine Association.

THE ONLY DOGGY HOUSE
IN THE TOWN.

*'Kennel Gazette' & all Fanciers' Papers taken.*

ALEX. FORBES,
Proprietor.

*A view of old Salford about 1880 with the White Bull Hotel on the right*

CHAPTER 10

# The White Bull Hotel

WHEN the lower portion of Railway Road was constructed soon after 1882, the River Blakewater was not only covered in but also diverted. It formerly struck across what is now the old parish churchyard, round the back of the White Bull Inn to a spot where a wooden footbridge formerly stood and thence took a wide sweep to join its present line at the foot of Jubilee Street. But even at the opening of last century its waters had lost their pristine purity.

This is what the editor of the *Blackburn Mail* had to say on the subject on September 12, 1804 : "We have lately observed the inhabitants of this town more than usually busy in fetching water from near the bridge, out of what at other times might be called a brook but from the dryness of the season cannot be deemed more than a stagnant ditch, most shockingly impregnated with the deleterious rinsings from a dyehouse close therto. Our information is that the water is purposely got for brewing, but as we have obtained a Police Act, if the Committee are too supine to attend to one essential matter, the health of the inhabitants, we think it our duty to point out to them their neglect . . ."

Yet in 1644 trees overshadowed its limped waters in the vicinity of the White Bull and there were trout playing about its clear, sandy shallows. In such surroundings the quaint old hotel, with its picturesque gables reflected in the peaceful waters, its courtyard overlooked by the yews in the ancient burial ground and its dusky corridors echoing to the sound of the old church bells, must have been a pleasant and inviting picture to the eye of the weary traveller.

It seems curious that the White Bull Hotel, which for so many centuries has stood beside Blackburn's medieval bridge, near the site of a still older ford undoubtedly used by Roman legionaries under the command of Agricola, should not have been one of the most important Blackburn coaching hotels. Yet, for some reason unknown, coaches passing over the bridge baited at the Bay Horse across the river.

Possibly the fact that, before the Blackburn Improvement Act of 1882, the street level was too high, may have some bearing on the matter. Salford Bridge was a typical narrow, hump-backed structure of the period and the approach from the west was so steep that one had to descend eight or nine steps to enter the old White Bull. In fact, it was said that passengers from the road were able to look in at the bedroom windows. In these circumstances it would be difficult, if not quite impossible, for a coach and four to draw up in front of the hotel.

Whatever the difficulty, however, it had been overcome before the coming of the railway in 1846, for at least one coach operated from the White Bull stables at the beginning of last century. It travelled daily from Howard's Black Bull in Clitheroe and was known as the Perseverance, the driver being a well-known character, "Neddy" Spencer. He drove the first Ribblesdale coach, which ran from the Brownlow Arms on Wednesdays and Saturdays.

R. Lang's map of Blackburn, which is dated 1739, reveals the White Bull detached and isolated, the nearest tenement in Church Street being some considerable distance westward. Before it was re-built in 1852, the fabric was early Jacobean of some distinction, with timber-framed gables and hooded mullion windows, deeply recessed.

The first reference I can trace is a statement printed in July, 1779, giving notice that a box left by Mr. Marlow, comedian, about three years previously, at the sign of the White Bull in Blackburn, and containing wearing apparel, would be sold to defray expenses, if not claimed within one month. From this brusque threat, it would seem that Mr. Marlow was one of a company of strolling players who visited the Theatre Royal about this period, often playing to scanty audiences and compelled through lack of funds to abscond without paying their hotel bills, perforce leaving behind their baggage, such as it was.

James Aspinall was tenant of the White Bull in 1793, when his wife died and he gave up the premises to Peter Pilkington, who held it for twelve years. His widow continued in possession until 1807, when she was succeeded by Robert Calvert and later John Briggs.

In Baines' Directory of 1824 the name of the landlord is given as William Greenwood, but by December 4th, 1833, he was dead and his widow was in possession. Her tenancy was marked by an incident which I transcribe from the Blackburn Alfred newspaper of that date:

"In the course of the night of Monday week a most daring burglary was committed on the premises of Mrs. Greenwood of the White Bull Inn, Salford Bridge. A gentleman named Yates, who travels with silk handkerchiefs, &c. had arrived at the house during the day and when he and the family had retired to rest, his packages were left in the back parlour. When the servants got up in the morning they were surprised to find a quantity of hay in the room and the traveller's packages lying open. It appeared that a pane of glass out of the window had been removed and silk handkerchiefs, tapes, &c. to the value of £7 stolen.

"Information of the robbery was immediately communicated to Mr. Kay and he forthwith set on foot the most active measures to apprehend the villains. It was ascertained that a silk handkerchief answering in description to some of those stolen, had been pawned at Mr. Normans, and in the course of Tuesday last Mr. Kay, with some of his assistants, visited the well-known thieves rendezvous, the cinder-ovens in Eanam and there apprehended two youths, one of whom, singularly enough, was sleeping wrapped in a horse-cloth which was stolen from Mrs. Greenwood's stable on Saturday week. They were subsequently brought before J. Feilden Esq., and gave their names as John McCann and Robert Hargreaves, and such evidence was given by Mr. Yates and others that on Saturday last they were both committed to the Preston House of Correction, for trial at the ensuing sessions."

The sequel is a grim commentary on the stringency of the Georgian penal code. For stealing a horse-blanket and a few articles of haberdashery, these two youths were both transported: McCann for life and Hargreaves for seven years. Indeed, the former was fortunate to escape being hanged.

*Old Northgate about 1860. The white gable of the Paganini Inn can be seen on the left, just behind the horse-drawn cab*

CHAPTER 11

# The Mason's Arms, Northgate

THE old Mason's Arms formerly stood facing two ways, one frontage being in Northgate and the other in Town Hall Street (then known as Thunder Alley), opposite the Girls' Charity School. The site is now occupied by the Blackburn Co-operative Society Emporium, but we may gather something of its orignal appearance from our illustration of Northgate in 1904, taken from a drawing by T. Robinson, which he made whilst standing on the footpath in front of the inn.

It began its career as a three-storied dwelling-house, its age being indicated by a dated downspout, "T.N.C. 1745" (Thomas and Catherine Nevill). This member of an old Blackburn family married in 1736 and probably erected the mansion as a town house. In its style it represented one of the better-class residences of the period. When first built, it would have been the last private house in Northgate, if not in the entire township on the north-west side, for the Girls' Charity School was not built until some twenty years later.

Northgate was notorious for its numerous taverns and hostelries, being contiguous to the ancient fair ground on Blakeley Moor. For this reason the thoroughfare was exceptionally wide, to make room for the carts and wains of the farmers at fair times and market days. This fact would account for the old house's conversion into an inn, just before the turn of the century. It was last occupied as a residence by a medical man, Dr. Joseph Lancaster, who in his day was a leading light among the congregation of St. Paul's Church, Nab Lane, which was demolished some years ago. Concerning this connection I have found a curious comment in the *Blackburn Mail.* In September, 1801, the church was advertised for sale by private contract, together with the churchyard. Although the period covered by the Napoleonic wars was not remarkable for its religious fervour, this notice was sufficiently unusual as to evoke some dry editorial comment:

"We do not know whether the churches of that description are under the same regulations as public houses, by being kept open until fresh tenants are provided but we learn that on Sunday last Dr. Lancaster ordered St. Paul's bell to be rung giving a notice of service. He then presented himself at the reading desk and read a part of the morning service, after which he ascended the pulpit and read a lecture or sermon there . . . He will not have a chance of marrying and if he buries, especially one of his patients, then our wags will swear he is hiding his bad work."

Despite this bold effort, however, St. Paul's, which was used by members of Lady Huntingdon's persuasion, was not admitted to the bosom of the Church of England until 1829. Nevertheless, the worthy doctor was a most enterprising man. Inheriting a parcel of land from his mother at Wensley Fold, he erected thereon what was probably the oldest spinning mill in the borough, for it was in operation in 1777, the machinery being actuated by a water-wheel. Here he later installed a number of Hargreave's Jennies, which within two years were the objects of a popular uprising, during which they were all destroyed.

According to tradition, this factory was the first to be lighted by gas in Blackburn, this being conveyed by road from Manchester in enormous bladders. The mill was also noted for its time signal, the famous Wensley Fold "Blunderbuss," which was fired by the watchman every night at 9 o'clock. This curious custom was subsequently adopted by the town council and Blackburn's one o'clock gun became an institution from 1878. The first piece, a home-made article, was presented to the town by Messrs. W. & J. Yates, ironfounders, and was originally sited on top of the town hall. Here it remained until 1883, when it was removed to a staging in the storeyard of the Highways Department.

The Mason's Arms must have been in existence before 1798, for in that year the *Blackburn Mail* reports a robbery when " . . . some villain or villains found means to conceal themselves in some part of the Mason's Arms at the upper end of Northgate, while the family were asleep, forced the till in the bar and absconded with some £60 in notes and silver."

Some curious circumstances attended the robbery, for a few nights later a letter was found containing one of the stolen notes, and threatening death to the landlord if he persisted in trying to trace the thieves. Mine host at the time was John Hall but what the sequel to the matter was we have no means of knowing.

Another noteworthy Blackburn innkeeper, who resided here for upwards of forty years, was Ralph Southworth, who claimed to be a lineal descendant of the Southworths of Samlesbury Hall.

The late John Lund said that in Southworth's time the Manchester piece buyers used to congregate at the Mason's Arms, where they were met by local handloom operators or "putters-out." The room in which they met was known significantly as the "brandy and water room."

Subsequent licensees included Thomas Briggs, who later built the Crown Hotel in Victoria Street; Jeremiah Thompson, who gave up inn-keeping in 1870 and embarked in the coal trade with the firm of Crook and

Thompson, building a villa at Hoghton, and finally John Hunter, at one time a noted football player in the Blackburn Olympic Club.

In an earlier article on Northgate's "pubs" I made a brief reference to its associations with the famous violinist Paganini and a correspondent has since asked if I have any further information about his visit. Curiously enough, little or nothing has been preserved in our local annals, so perhaps I may close this somewhat discursive article by quoting some original notes in my possession. In 1833 he agreed to give a single concert in the Theatre Royal in Blackburn on September 5th, coming from Bolton for that purpose. His arrival was marked by a calamity, for on descending from the stage coach he dropped his precious violin, damaging the finger-board. However, the damage was temporarily repaired and he duly appeared, including in his repertoire variations on the Canzonetta, "The Carnival of Venice" and Sonata Militaire, entirely on the G string.

"The sight of Paganini (wrote an eye-witness) as he emerged from one of the stage wings was very disappointing to me. In place of the fine gentleman I had been led to expect I beheld a shabbily-dressed man with a slouching gait and a downcast countenance. He advanced with head downwards, utterly oblivious of the great applause which greeted his appearance and dragging the bow of his violin on the floor. The first note produced quite made my hair stand on end, so different was it in grandeur to anything I had ever heard before. Paganini had his audience spellbound from the first note and as he proceeded with his theme the tears began to trickle down his cheeks."

*Old Salford Bridge with the Bay Horse Inn on the far bank*

CHAPTER 12

# The Bay Horse Inn

ALTHOUGH, in an earlier article dealing with old Penny Street, I made a passing reference to the Bay Horse Inn, I think this fine old hostelry (now, alas, no more) was of sufficient importance in the town's annals as to deserve another article to itself. For one thing, its unique position, dominating the old town centre and keeping watch, as it were, over the narrow medieval bridge and ford at Salford, made it the focal point of Blackburn's social activities for many years.

Here, for example, the famous Salford Bridge Committee had its headquarters. According to legend, this formidable junta, consisting of many of the town's prominent citizens, conducted most of its deliberations leaning over the parapet of the old bridge. Here, prior to the township's Incorporation in 1851 and the formation of the first town council, matters normally dealt with by the Improvement Commissioners were debated and, after a course of action had been decided upon, their decree was issued and woe betide the Commissioners if they refused to act upon it. Among the members of the Committee were Joseph Haydock, spirit merchant; Edward Holroyd, sizer; Thomas Ainsworth, tailor; Thomas Lister, tinplate worker; and Adam Balshaw, plumber. After their business for the day was completed, the Committee adjourned to their council-room in the Bay Horse bar parlour and presumably drank to the success of their labours.

For some time the inn was largely patronised by Blackburn Conservatives and it was from here that they conducted their campaign during the town's first parliamentary election after the passing of the Reform Act in 1832. During the election riots of 1835, W. H. Hornby (later Blackburn's charter mayor), who was the sponsor of one of the elected members, was flung over the parapet of old Salford Bridge. Dr. Bowring, the reformer and popular candidate, had been defeated and in this way the town's radical element gave vent to their displeasure. Hornby and some of his colleagues were just emerging from the back door of the Bay Horse when they were surrounded by the mob and he himself thrown into the mud on the easterly side of the bridge.

The late Charles Haworth, whose pen-drawing of the bridge is so well-known, recalled as a youth rescuing the victim from his predicament and helping to brush down his clothes whilst he purchased a new beaver hat at Dack's shop across the way. He records that the great man took his ducking "very complacently." After all, his man had got in, and that was the thing that really mattered.

The Bay Horse was also associated with the formation of Blackburn's first newspaper, the *Blackburn Mail,* founded by J. Waterworth in 1793, the first edition appearing on May 29th. Earlier in the year he called a meeting of prospective subscribers in the Bay Horse, this being the nearest hostelry to his office. Adjoining the inn on the east side of Water Street was a row of ancient tenements known as God's Providence Row and it was in one of these that the "*Mail*" first saw the light of day. Many years later, when the old house was demolished, the workmen were astonished to find many pieces of type lying under the floor-boards. Compositors are notoriously a thirsty race and there is little doubt that, when they laboured during the watches of the night, many a foaming tankard from the neighbouring inn helped to stimulate their mental processes.

Joseph Hanby took over the editorship in 1807 and in 1821 the proprietress was his widow Elizabeth, with her office in Fleming Square. Her husband was the son of the Rev. Thomas Hanby, one of the earliest ministers of the Wesleyan connexion and a companion of John Wesley. Although the "*Mail*" was a Tory organ, Hanby's predecessor was guilty of some strange lapses, one of the most glaring being to print the French version of the battle of Trafalgar alongside the official despatch. As the French account claims the victory for the French Admiral Villeneuve, who, during the course of the battle, is alleged to have boarded the Victory and shot Nelson with his own hand, one can understand something of the prejudice Hanby had to live down.

Under his guidance, however, the paper quickly improved until it became the leading weekly journal in East Lancashire. In 1813 he records, in happier vein, the rejoicings over the news of Wellington's victories in the Peninsular, when " . . . the bells of our venerable church rang a merry peal" and an effigy of Bonaparte was " . . . publicly burned in the Market Place." Today the curious pilgrim may still meditate beside his quiet resting-place in the shadow of St. John's Church, where there is a stone, now somewhat time-worn, to the memory of "Joseph Hanby, eleven years editor of the *Blackburn Mail.*"

In the early years of last century Salford was a veritable bottleneck. The corner shop of Dack the hatter projected beyond the parapet of the old hump-backed bridge and with the Bay Horse on the opposite side, narrowed the approach to less than twenty-two feet. The entrance to Penny Street was similarly hemmed-in and there was a blind corner where Hallows Spring Lane, skirting the river on the other side, opened out on the bridge-end. The whole area was little more than a warren of narrow, winding entries, ginnels and alleyways, an ideal haunt for thieves and juvenile delinquents, of which the town had its fair share.

When the old bridge was first widened in 1846, the Bay Horse Inn, together with the adjoining hostelry popularly termed the Roundabout (later the Lord Nelson but at that time displaying the sign of the Bull's Head), were set back some fifty feet and re-erected in the substantial early-Victorian style.

Although the old inn's coaching activities date back to 1793, when J. Castree inaugurated a service between Blackburn and Manchester, inside fare 8s.; outside 4s. 6d., it was also the main depot for the Clitheroe run. A coach left the stable-yard (which had accommodation for over thirty horses) daily, this being either the "Hark Forward" or the "Tally Ho." The driver of the one was John Cowell, an old steeplechase rider, and the return fare was 2s. These coaches also carried the mails, thus superseding the original postboy, who rode on horseback, with the mail bags across the front of the saddle.

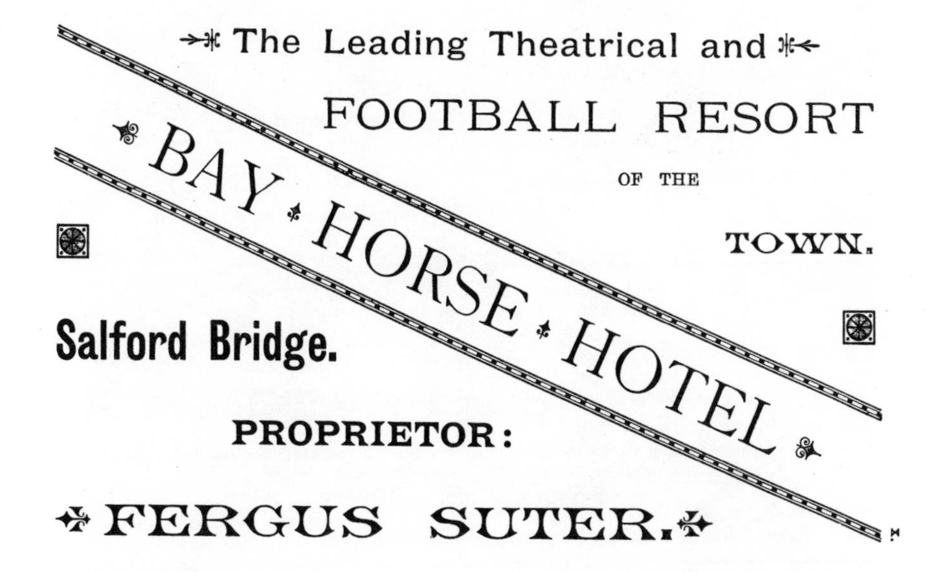

*Pleasington Old Hall, the family seat of the Ainsworths*

CHAPTER 13

# The Dun Horse Inn

IT is surprising how many of Blackburn's older inns have their roots buried deep in the past. Some we know could trace their origin as far back as the 17th century and, until the last decade, stood like landmarks in the rushing stream of time, to remind us of more serene days. If one of our early-Victorian forebears were permitted to return awhile to the once familiar scenes of his childhood, I have no doubt he would be greatly impressed and overawed at the speed and efficiency of modern existence; its aspiring structures of steel and concrete; its rushing, stream-lined traffic and its ruthless commercialism: he would admire our central heating, our electrically-controlled domestic appliances, our sophistication and our general air of well-being. But whether he would envy us is quite another matter. A single glance at our newspaper headlines and he might well be glad to crawl back under his tombstone, if it is still standing.

We know that the Dun Horse Inn, which formerly stood at the Darwen Street end of Market Street Lane, was in existence in 1715, from the evidence of a contemporary tract written during the first Jacobite rebellion. From it we know that while the rebel army lay at Preston, one Captain Douglas made a sally as far as Balderston in search of arms and horses for the Pretender's forces. Finding none available he took the rash step of entering Blackburn in the guise of a traveller.

Unfortunately for him, as it transpired, the townsfolk were alert and under the leadership of Captain Ainsworth, of Pleasington, had armed themselves with guns, clubs and pikes, while the Rev. John Holme conducted public prayers in the parish church for the welfare of the reigning monarch. Douglas called at the Dun Horse Inn, hoping to hear something of the movements of the Hanoverian forces but being recognised for a spy, he was compelled to beat a hasty retreat and was lucky to escape with his life.

I find the first local reference to this old hostelry in the *Blackburn Mail* for December 2nd, 1795, when T. Butler begged leave "to inform his friends that he has opened his warehouse in Market Street Lane adjoining the Dun Horse." On December 9th, 1801, the same journal contains the following news item: "Mare rode away with. Whereas on Tuesday the 1st inst. a man of about 18 or 19 years of age, dark complexion and black hair, in a bottle-green close coat, yellow-striped waistcoat and brown top coat, engaged at the Dun Horse in this town a mare, the property of Mr. Thomas Blundell, as he said, to go to Preston and return on Wednesday, but has not yet been heard of. The mare is a very dark grey . . . and rather given to swelling in the legs and has a method when rode of scowling or putting her ears back."

At that time the landlord was Robert Wood, who in June, 1802, was succeeded by Stephen Parker, formerly mine host of the White Bull, Salford Bridge. It is during his tenancy that we are given the first intimation of its use as a posting house. This is revealed in another news item of October 27th, 1802. "A famous traveller. Mr. Wyndham is on a tour of observation at present: on Saturday in the evening he arrived at the Dun Horse in this town, accompanied by only one gentleman for the purpose of drawing views, &c., one servant with a close carriage and a phaeton, taking post horse Mr. W. condescendingly entered into conversation with Mr. S. Parker the landlord for upwards of an hour, and asked various questions relative to the trade, &c. of this place and neighbourhood."

Henry Penruddock Wyndham was a noted topographer of the day and author of several books, including "A Gentleman's Tour through Monmouthshire and Wales in 1774." The above news item gave rise to some controversy, for on the following week the editor makes a tart comment: "One of our contemporaries, mentioning Mr. Wyndham having passed through the town, observes that from the flourishing state of commerce in that place at present, compared with its perishing situation during the war and hopes the journey will be useful to him in correcting some of his views. With regard to the words "perishing state of commerce" &c. we beg leave to put the gentleman right in that particular, by informing him it could by no means be applied to this place, as the trade of the town more than doubled during the late war nor was there occasion in that period for anyone to be idle for want of employment, whose disposition led them to work and although since the peace (if it yet merits that name) a far greater number of hands are seemingly unemployed, we very much query whether a greater number of pieces of calico have been made last year . . . "

Parker did not preside over the inn's destiny for long, for in May, 1805, it was advertised "To be let by ticket," present occupier John Hall. The extent of its posting activities may be judged from the fact that it possessed stabling for sixteen horses, with other out-buildings. Although close to the old market place it was hemmed in by narrow streets and so hardly likely to attain the status of a coaching inn. Both Mincing Lane (then known as Back Lane) and Mill Lane were quite unsuitable for the quick passage of a lively four-horse team of stage coach horses. According to Baines, a carrier's wagon left the Dun Horse yard in 1824 for Preston and Kirkham every Tuesday morning, whilst others owned by John Smith left daily for Manchester and Chorley. Exemplifying the narrowness of the streets, there is a news item the following year describing an accident involving one of these wagons, which, whilst turning into Mill Lane, completely demolished a smithy at the corner.

In 1825 the landlady was Mary Weall, but on August 23rd, 1826, James Holding, who describes himself as living at the Dun Horse, gave the following evidence at Lancaster Assizes during the trial of the Blackburn loom-breaking rioters. Its intimate details are worth repeating:

"I live at the Dun Horse. I was at the factory (the Dandy Factory in Jubilee Street). I had just got at the gates of the mill when I saw Thomas Dickinson there; he was amongst those who had burst the gates open. I heard him say: 'Stand back; let's come.' This he said to the rest of the mob. The mob was then in great numbers about the gates; there were some nearer the gates than he was when he said so. I saw him go into the yard and then going towards the factory door. There were many persons going with him at the time; there were several hundreds there. I am sure he is the man. I have known him twelve months; he usually sells toffy about the streets."

It is satisfactory to record that on such flimsy evidence the jury found the prisoner: Not Guilty.

Here I have recalled just a few disconnected incidents in the story of just one old tavern, incidents garnered from the stubble of the years and stored away haphazard. Only a fragmentary tale, but sufficient to reveal the wealth of material once available but now lost for ever. Some day we may have cause to regret this wanton dissipation of our township's scanty archives.

*The Spread Eagle Inn situated in Cable Street*

CHAPTER 14

# The Spread Eagle

CABLE Street and the foundations of Cable House have long been obliterated from the face of modern Blackburn, to make way for the austere facade of our new market. Steel and concrete superimpose what was once a modern Georgian purlieu adjoining the town centre and today nothing remains but a memory and a tradition.

Tradition says that the street's curious name derived from the fact that there was once an ancient rope-walk on the site but for once tradition lies. The truth is that the house was erected by a member of the Cable family, from whom it, and in later years the street itself, derived their name. One of the last of the line, a naval midshipman, was drowned at sea during the Napoleonic wars and shortly afterwards the property passed into the hands of the Ainsworths, also commemorated by a street name in the vicinity.

At the beginning of last century, when Cable House was new, it stood in its own grounds, which extended along both banks of the Blakewater almost to Salford Bridge. It is on record that an arched rustic bridge crossed what was then a clear, unpolluted stream dancing on its way through fresh, green lawns and carefully-tended flower beds, the cheerful tinkle as it rippled over pebbled cascades, echoing among secluded walks shaded by over-arching trees and hidden by clumps of rhododendrons.

The house was not a large one and did not pretend to vie with the mansions of the Hornbys and the Cardwells in King Street but it was infinitely better sited and had a pleasant air of gentility, enhanced by a graceful porch supported by slender pillars.

Here, during the abortive peace celebrations of 1801, the *Blackburn Mail* records that Joseph Ainsworth illuminated his grounds with coloured lanterns festooned among the trees, forming " . . . a petit Vauxhall, where the military band attended and the dance, with everything expressive of a fete champetre, enlivened the hearts of all who were happy to obtain admittance."

Again, on the occasion of the jubilee of George III, he hoisted a large flag from the roof of the mansion and in the evening gave an exhibition of fireworks. When he died, however, the house lost its importance, being used for some time as a surgery by Doctor Barlow and later as a lock-up by the town constable.

By 1811, however, it had become the Spread Eagle Inn, as was intimated by a huge carved figure raised high above the apex of the gable. Actually, the bird thus depicted was not an eagle at all, but a phoenix, rising, as the legend avers, from its own ashes, and originally it must have graced the premises of some progressive fire assurance company. However, as few of the tavern's habitues were ornithologists, it served its purpose just as well. What a pity it did not survive as a symbol to embellish the entrance to our new market.

Some idea of the old inn's accommodation may be obtained from a notice which appeared in the *Blackburn Mail* dated November 27th, 1811: "To be sold. All that old-established and well-accustomed inn or public house, known by the sign of the Spread Eagle, situate on the north side of Penny Street, within Blackburn, with large backyard, an excellent brew-house, stabling for five horses, a shippon for two cows and several out-rooms to such inn, belonging and adjoining, and now in the possession of Mr. John Hall."

Its appearance during this later stage of its existence may be judged by the illustration, which is a faithful record of the old place as I remember it in my youth. But like most secluded taverns, cut off from the busy town centre by a maze of narrow alleys, the Spread Eagle had its own particular patrons. For some years it was the meeting-place of a friendly society and at one time it bade fair to rival the Poet's Corner pub in Bradshaw Street as the haunt of many of our local bards.

These robust minstrels played a great part in the cultural life of Blackburn at the outset of the Industrial Revolution and it was in such snug little haunts as the Spread Eagle that they foregathered to iron out their many problems and, if need be, settle their differences over a friendly tankard of ale. They had a glorious precedent, for was not rare Ben Jonson and William Shakespeare among the goodly company that frequented the Mermaid Tavern in Elizabethan London, oft (alas) carousing until the early hours.

When Dr. Skinner, pastor of Mount Street Chapel, opened the Rechabites Hall just across the way, it must have been a sad blow to mine host of the Spread Eagle. According to local legend, he registered his protest in a somewhat novel manner by bribing some inveterate enemy of teetotalism to pour croton oil in the opposition tea urn at the height of their opening festivities. He was never brought to justice, although a reward of five pounds was offered for his discovery.

After catering to the wants of the inner man for well-nigh a century, the old inn lost its licence some time before 1909, and when the area was cleared, it was one of the first buildings to go. The shell of its old rival, the Rechabites Hall, lingered a little longer but finally bowed to the inevitable. In this fashion time ends all antagonisms and issues. Vital to one generation they are forgotten by the next, unless some prosy local historian, poring over his dusty files, can make these dry bones live once more, if only for a day.

*A well-known picture of Blackburn Market Cross in 1715, showing the Old Bull Inn with the parish church in the background*

CHAPTER 15

# The Old Bull Inn

THIS fine old inn (whose final obliteration was much deplored) was of such significance in the social history of Blackburn township that I feel I cannot do better than conclude my survey of our ancient hostelries with some further details. Actually, I have enough material in my notes concerning this one inn to make a substantial book, a veritable pageant of our history as it marched through the centuries in colourful procession past those hospitable doors.

I could not pretend to say when the Old Black Bull hostelry (to give it its proper title) was founded. Over five hundred years ago, certainly, but how much further back in the dim corridors of time we shall never know. It was probably coeval with the old water mill of the Lord of the Ville, and it is shown by charters that there was such a mill in the township six hundred years ago, on a site adjoining the old grammar school in Freckleton Street.

But this venerable inn had another reason for its existence. In those early times Blackburn parish church was the mother church for an area extending from the banks of the Ribble to the summit of the moors above Darwen and from the boundary of Rishton to the Pleasington demesne. Obviously the stout yeomen of this wide tract of country, whether the occasion of their visit was a christening, a wedding or a funeral, the celebration of some church festival or just an ordinary service, would require stabling for their horses and refreshment for themselves and their families. And where better than an inn on the very threshold of the church itself?

As one half of Blackburn manor, including the church and advowson, was held by the monks of Whalley until the Dissolution, the inn probably owes its origin to that fraternity. Doubtless the monks who officiated as vicars resided at the abbey and had a chamber in the inn reserved for their use when they rode over from Whalley. At least there is no proof that a vicarage stood in the churchyard until after the Reformation.

By the close of the reign of the first Elizabeth, we know that two or three other hostelries had been established. From the parish registers of the 17th century, we find the following records: John Siddall of Blackburn, innkeeper, died in 1636; William Yates, died in 1660; James Ainsworth, died in 1664; Ellis Edge, died in 1669; Richard Gillibrand, died in 1692; Richard Sharples, 1697 and Henry Astley, who died before 1721. Of these we know that Richard Sharples was mine host of the Bull, for it was in his house that the justices of the district assembled, and this was the principal inn at which a court-house was provided. During the Civil War it would be here that the grim Puritan justices issued their orders for the demolition of the old market cross and the destruction of the idolatrous image of Judge Walmsley on his tomb in the Dunkenhalgh Chapel of the parish church. But in those stirring times the tide of battle ebbed and flowed and when the town was captured by the Royalists under Prince Rupert, there is little doubt that roistering troopers and pikemen would take their revenge on the ale maturing in the inn cellars in cask and hogshead. Nevertheless, it is recorded that Master William Yates, inn-keeper, was appointed quartermaster in Blackburn. This would give him the opportunity of billeting the Parliamentary levies in the various hostelries that had suffered most from Royalist depredations and so enable them to recoup their losses.

Among the names of tenants of Blackburn Rectory (70 in number) inscribed on the curious map of the demesne made in 1739, the first tenement named is the Black Bull, then held by Thomas Johnson, who also held a parcel of rectorial glebe known as "Dixon's." He died soon after this date and his successor, in occupation before 1754, was John Yates. He, and his son William, are the most interested townfolk associated with the Bull, because of their personal relations with the Peel family. Doubtless the William Yates already referred to above, who died in 1660, would be an ancestor.

For many years the lessee of the rectorial estate held his rent audit at the "Bull," for in the book of accounts kept by John Bolton is the item: "1748. Paid John Yates for ale given to the tenants when they paid their Christmas rent, 3s. 4d." He was one of the original members of the Blackburn Subscription Bowling Green established in 1753 in the vicinity of Mount Street and after his retirement in 1772 he served the club for one year as steward and honorary treasurer. It was his son William who became a partner with the elder Robert Peel in the firm of Haworth, Peel and Yates, calico printers. His daughter, Ellen, baptised in the parish church on April 2nd, 1766, subsequently became the wife of Sir Robert Peel, the first baronet.

Samuel Rixon became tenant of the old "Black Bull' inn towards the end of 1769 for 18 years, the residue of the Yates' lease. He is occasionally named in the rectory accounts: "1770. August 3rd. Paid Mr. Samuel Rixon for licquor had with Mr. John Feilden and Mr. Henry Heaton on account of the dispute with Abbot and others concerning a seat in the chancell (of the parish church), 3s. 4d." "1778. Pd. Mr. Samuel Rixon's bill and others for the expenses attending the letting of the Tythes of Blackburn Parish, £6.13s."

In an amusing piece of local satire entitled: "The History of Robin Foo'," poor simple Robin was directed to procure some barm in exchange for eggs at the Black Bull. He was to proceed to the Market Cross, "an' just o'er anenst it an' on th'other side o' Whalley's gret heawse (on the site of the present Old Bank) tha'll see a Black Bull atop of a pow." This was in Rixon's time and the point of the story is that Robin mistook his mother's description of the old inn, with its great chimney built up to the gable end, for the parish church and marched up the aisle in the middle of a service to ask the vicar for some barm. But whether the inn sign was a rude wooden figure of a bull (like that of the White Bull still to be seen at Ribchester) or a board with a bull painted thereon and swinging at the end of a pole, we have no means of knowing.

The fabric of the ancient hostelry, having braved the storms of many centuries, was demolished and re-built in 1847, the work being expedited by the action of the Improvement Commissioners in laying out the streets at the Cross upon a better system, with altered levels. The old footpaths were narrow and irregular and the north-east gable of the inn projected far into the street. In the new erection it was proposed that two projecting flights of stone steps should be removed, that the building should be rounded at the corner and set back to make a seven-feet wide path in Darwen Street.

For some time, both before and after the re-building, the Old Bull flags served as a meeting-place or Exchange for prominent Blackburn cotton merchants and at "high change" between 3 and 5 p.m. on Wednesdays they might be seen standing before the main entrance discussing market fluctuations. This was continued until 1857, when the Exchange was shifted to the town hall vestibule.

In the intervening years, prior to its final demolition in 1950 the old inn had many other landlords and saw many vicissitudes. I have not the space to record them here but the material, together with much else relating to bygone Blackburn, is still available. Maybe in the distant future there may arise in the township a body sufficiently public-spirited to publish them for the benefit of posterity.

**Mrs. Mitchell, "Old Bull" Commercial and Family Hotel,** Church Street, Blackburn.—To the commercial gentleman visiting distant parts the hotel is an institution of the utmost importance, and it is therefore appropriate in these reviews of our industries to make prominent mention of a thoroughly representative hotel in Blackburn. Such we have in that of the "Old Bull" Commercial and Family Hotel, which is situated in Church Street. Founded half a century ago, the "Old Bull" was rebuilt thirty years ago, and is the property of Mrs. Mitchell, who has occupied it for the last ten years. This house, which is the foremost and most popular commercial and family hotel in Blackburn, consists of a handsome square building of three storeys in height, and measuring 100 feet square. On the ground floor there are commercial room, coffee room, private sitting rooms, billiard room, four stock rooms, and bar and parlour; the floor above having upwards of forty bedrooms, a spacious dining hall nearly occupying the whole of the upper floor. Every room is handsomely furnished, and there being twenty servants, first-class fare, moderate charges, and a most agreeable, courteous hostess, commercial gentlemen and private families at once find themselves at home in the "Old Bull," whose omnibus meets all trains for the convenience of guests coming or going.

# Blackburn's Licensed Houses in 1893

by Bob Dobson

As early as 1861, the thirty-years old Blackburn Temperance Society was complaining that there were too many drinking establishments in the town - then there were 164 fully-licensed houses (selling spirits as well as beer) and 284 beer-only houses. This total had increased since the Police Superintendent reported in 1849 on the 112 fully-licensed houses and the 176 beerhouses. It was estimated that, in 1860, £162,368 was spent on intoxicants in Blackburn, and in that year 85 licensees appeared before the local magistrates, who heard 1,198 cases of drunkenness. In that year, the Police Superintendent reported to the magistrates, quoting the words of the chaplain to the Preston House of Correction -"*The evil wrought in such a singing room on a single night outweighs all the good that can be affected by a dozen Sunday Schools in a year.*"

In 1863, a leading Temperance worker, Mrs Mary Bayly visited Blackburn to see for herself the atrocious social conditions brought about by drink. She posed the question "*What ails Blackburn?*" The answer was - "*Ale ails Blackburn*".

In 1890, Reverend Moffett, vicar of Holy Trinity Church, spoke up over the excessive number of licensed houses "*on behalf of the people and the poor, who have been treated under the present abuse of licences as if they were of no account, as if they were only born to be ruined.*" In his parish there was a licensed house for every hundred inhabitants, and he believed there was a link between crime and beerhouses. Clearly, the magistrates took these views on board, for they ordered a survey of the borough's 495 pubs and off-licensed houses (where intoxicants could be sold only for consumption *off* the premises). This was done in 1893, and the list which follows is from that survey. Note that several pubs had the same name, and that many were very close to the next one - mostly less than 100 yards. The spellings are as used in 1893.

One result of the survey was that, at the next Brewster (Licensing) Sessions, the number was reduced by 24.

## Licensed Houses in Blackburn in 1893

F=Fully Licensed B=Beerhouse

1. Castle Hotel, 1 Great Bolton Street, and 2 Park Road (F)
2. Ostler's Arms, 17 Great Bolton Street (B)
3. Tramway Hotel, 33 Great Bolton Street (F)
4. Volunteers' Arms, 43 Great Bolton Street (B)
5. Gardeners' Inn, 49 Great Bolton Street (F)
6. Carters' Arms, 55 Great Bolton Street (B)
7. Brewers' Arms, Great Bolton Street (F)
8. Weavers' Arms, 1 Bolton Road (F)
9. Old Industrious Bee, 75 Great Bolton Street (B)
10. Globe Inn, 30, Park Road (F)
11. Nelson Inn, 26, 28 Park Road (F)
12. Quarryman's Arms, 50 Park Road (F)
13. Anglo Saxon, 17 Howard Street (B)
14. Industrious Bee, 28 & 30 Bolton Road (F)
15. New Brewery Inn, 49 Bolton Road (B)
16. Spinners' Arms, 57 Bolton Road (B)
17. Welcome Inn, 59 Bolton Road (B)
18. Heights of Alma, 91, 93 Bolton Road (B)
19. Sweet Willow, 62 Bolton Road (B)
20. Cheetham Arms, 111, 113, Bolton Road (B)
21. Oddfellows Arms, 7 Commercial Street (B)
22. Crown Inn, 127 Bolton Road (F)
23. Oak Tavern, 27 Troop Street (B)
24. Fruits of Industry, 40 Kay Street (B)
25. Nelson's Monument, 38 Kay Street (B)
26. Harrison's Arms Hotel, 82, 84 Bolton Road (F)
27. Sharples Arms, 92, 94 Bolton Road (B)
28. Commercial Inn, 96 Bolton Road (F)
29. Druids' Arms, 19, 21 Sharples Street (B)
30. Carriers' Arms, 28 Sharples Street (B)
31. Horse Load Inn, 106 Bolton Road (F)
32. Off License, 19 and 21 Black Diamond Street
33. Infirmary Hotel, 197 Bolton Road (F)
34. Ivy Inn, 65 Infirmary Street (F)
35. Rockcliffe Inn, 44 Highfield Road (B)
36. Royal Oak, 60 Highfield Road (B)
37. Atlantic Hotel, 36 Mosley Street (F)
38. Harrison's Arms, 28 Mosley Street (B)
39. Pilkington Arms, 35 Lower Audley Street (F)

40. Cambridge Hotel, 83 Lower Audley Street (F)
41. Off License, 100 Park Road
42. Victoria Inn, 29 Hutchinson Street (B)
43. Good Samaritan, 2 Grimshaw Park (F)
44. Prince of Wales Inn, 1 Grimshaw Park (F)
45. Royal Albert, 2 and 4, Friday Street (B)
46. Rose Bud, 11 Grimshaw Park (B)
47. Sebastopol Inn, 23 Friday Street (F)
48. Cross Guns, 13 Grimshaw Park (B)
49. Lamb and Lion, 14 Grimshaw Park and 2 St. Ann Street (B)
50. Auld Lang Syne, 38 and 40 Friday Street (B)
51. Carters' Arms, 9 Shorrock Street (B)
52. North Fleet, Shorrock Street (B)
53. Bridge Inn, 33 Grimshaw Park (F)
54. Clifton Arms, 48 Grimshaw Park (B)
55. Fishmongers' Inn, 76 Grimshaw Park (B)
56. Highfield Inn, 37 Grimshaw Park (F)
57. Queen's Park Inn, 39 Grimshaw Park (B)
58. Who Could a Thought It, 82 Grimshaw Park (B)
59. Turner's Arms, 51 Grimshaw Park (F)
60. Roast Beef Inn, 88, 90 Grimshaw Park (B)
61. Nope Inn, 53 Grimshaw Park (B)
62. Turk's Head Inn, 57 Grimshaw Park (F)
63. Spring View, 2 Haslingden Road (B)
64. Duke of Wellington, 1 Kemp Street (B)
65. Hutchinson's Arms, 45 Rockcliffe Street (F)
66. Robin Hood Inn, 57 Haslingden Road (F)
67. Rock Inn, 69 Haslingden Road (B)
68. Stop and Rest, 188 Brandy House Brow (B)
69. Pleasant View Inn, 1 and 2 Roman Road (B)
70. Observatory Inn, 67 Whinney Edge (F)
71. Sett End, Shadsworth Road (B)
72. Cross Guns, 300 Haslingden Road (B)
73. Black Horse Inn, 390, 392 Haslingden Road (B)
74. Guide Inn, 327 Haslingden Road (F)
75. Original Guide Pole House Inn, 396 Haslingden Road (F)
76. Blackamoor Inn, 140 Roman Road (F)
77. Hindles Arms, 18 Rake's Bridge (F)
78. Railway Hotel, 1 Rake's Bridge (B)
79. Swan Inn, 27 Fore Street (F)
80. Off License, 468 Bolton Road
81. Fox and Hounds, 1 Ewood Brow (F)
82. Albion Hotel, 200 Bolton Road (F)

83. Aqueduct Inn, 83 Ewood Bridge (F)
84. Brown Cow Inn, Livesey Branch Road (F)
85. Moorgate Arms, 168 Livesey Branch Road (B)
86. White Bull, 3 Wellington Road (B)
87. Farmer's Boy, 93 Heys Lane (B)
88. Livesey New Inn, 1 Waterloo (F)
89. Lord Raglan Hotel, King's Road (F)
90. Wellington Inn, 362 Wellington Road (F)
91. King's Fold Inn, King's Fold, Livesey (B)
92. Navigation Inn, Canal Street (F)
93. Off License, 32, 34 Angelia Street, Livesey
94. Off License, 1 Francis Street and 86 Chapel Street
95. Stakes Hotel, 12 Albert Street (F)
96. Hamilton Arms, 1 Hollin Street (F)
97. Off License, 3 Hamilton Street
98. Swan Inn, 3 and 5 Astley Gate (F)
99. Sun Inn, 1 Astley Gate (F)
100. Lower Sun Inn, 4 Church Street (F)
101. Edinburgh Hotel, 6 Fleming Square (F)
102. Princes of Wales Inn, 15 Church Street (F)
103. Castle Inn, 4 and 6 Market St. Lane (F)
104. Dun Horse Inn, 13 Market Street Lane (F)
105. Standard of Unity, 20 Mincing Lane (B)
106. Wheat Sheaf Hotel, 23 Mincing Lane (F)
107. Eagle and Child Hotel, 18 Darwen Street (F)
108. George Inn, 82 Darwen Street (F)
109. Duke of York, 136 Darwen Street (F)
110. Stokers' Arms, 6 Islington (B)
111. Islington Tavern, 1 Pembroke Street (B)
112. Cattle Market Hotel, Harrison Street (F)
113. Prince Arthur Hotel, 65 Canterbury Street (F)
114. Crown Inn, 9 Cardwell Place (B)
115. Old Bank Hotel, 6 Mincing Lane (F)
116. Angel Inn, 6 and 8 King Street (F)
117. Sudell Hotel, 33 King Street (F)
118. Royal Hotel, 36, 38 King Street (F)
119. King's Head Inn, 43 King Street (F)
120. Montague Arms, 64 King Street (F)
121. Shakespeare Inn, 11 Montague Street and 1 Bent Street (B)
122. Pet Dog, 63 King Street (B)
123. Palatine Hotel, 72, 74 King Street (F)
124. Afghan Inn, 18 Whalley Banks (B)
125. Wellington Inn, 71 King Street (F)

126. Royal Oak Inn, 85 King Street (F)
127. Commercial Inn, 104 King Street (F)
128. Welcome Inn, 15 Bent Street (B)
129. Spindlemakers' Arms, 45 William Henry Street (B)
130. Prince of Wales Inn, 112 King Street (B)
131. White Dog, 2 Pearson Street (B)
132. Tower Inn, 23 Pearson Street (B)
133. Moss Rose, 74, 76 Chapel Street (B)
134. Farmer's Arms, 93, 95 Chapel Street (B)
135. Spring Vale Inn, 44, 46 Chapel Street (B)
136. Mitre Inn, 43 Chapel Street (F)
137. Phoenix Tavern, 120 King Street (B)
138. Forrester's Arms, 6 Whalley Banks (B)
139. Bridge Inn, 7 Whalley Banks (F)
140. Craven Heifer Inn, 3 Brunswick Street (B)
141. Oddfellows Arms, 23 Whalley Banks (F)
142. Boys of Harmony, 31, 33, Whalley Banks (B)
143. Postman's Arms, 20, 22 Brunswick Street (B)
144. Red House or The House that Jack Built, 41 Whalley Banks (B)
145. Royal Edward, 26 Whalley Banks (B)
146. Robin Hood Inn, 38, 40 Whalley Banks (B)
147. Primrose Inn, 52 Whalley Banks (B)
148. Railway Inn, 55 Whalley Banks (B)
149. Dun House, 63 Whalley Banks (B)
150. Tapers' Arms, 65 Whalley Banks (B)
151. Minders' Arms, 74, 76 Brunswick Street (B)
152. Pump House Inn, 76 Whalley Banks (F)
153. Rose Bud, 78 Whalley Banks (B)
154. Brown Dog, 5 Duckworth Street (B)
155. Black Swans, 17 Pump Street (F)
156. Sir Colin Campbell, 25, 27 Duckworth Street (B)
157. Off License, 55 Duckworth Street
158. London & North Western Hotel, 32 Galligreaves Street (F)
159. Off License, 34, 36 Galligreaves Street
160. Off License, 37 Taylor Street
161. Harrison Arms, 93 Taylor Street (F)
162. Havelock Inn, 1 Havelock Street (F)
163. Yutick's Nest, 41 Dickinson Street (B)
164. Shakespeare Hotel, 7 Bank Top (F)
165. Lord Byron Arms Hotel, 18, 20 Wellesley Street (F)
166. Foundry Arms, 24 Radcliffe Street (B)
167. Derby's Arms, 18 Bank Top (B)
168. Prince Albert, 27 Bank Top (B)

169. Brown Cow Inn, 74 Bank Top (B)
170. Turner's Arms, 82 Bank Top (F)
171. Red Lion Inn, 53, 55 Bank Top (B)
172. Unicorn, 84 Bank Top (B)
173. Weavers' Arms, 15 Throstle Street (B)
174. Wellwisher's Arms, 92, 94 Bank Top (B)
175. Corporation Arms, 116 Bank Top (F)
176. Off-license, 23, 25 Dixon Street
177. West View Inn, 9 West Street and 16 Howarth Street (B)
178. Farmers Arms, 130 Bank Top (B)
179. Boundary Arms, 138, 140 Bank Top (B)
180. Vegetable Arms, 2 Redlam Brow (B)
181. Stanley Arms, 1 Garden Street (F)
182. Off License, 2, 4 Lancaster Street
183. Off License, 67, 69 Garden Street
184. Griffin Inn, 2 Griffin Street (F)
185. Off License, 27, 29 Redlam
186. Bull's Head Inn, 63 Redlam (F)
187. Vauxhall Inn, 107 Redlam (F)
188. Witton Inn, 182 Witton Stocks (B)
189. Britannia Inn, 33, 35 Lord Street (F)
190. Stanley Arms, 20 Northgate (F)
191. Paganini Inn, 29 Northgate (F)
192. Nags Head Inn, 44, 46 Northgate (F)
193. King's Arms Inn, 31 Northgate (F)
194. Half Moon Inn, 35 Northgate (F)
195. George and Dragon Hotel, 62 Northgate (F)
196. Black Horse Inn, 41 Northgate (F)
197. Off License, 70 Northgate
198. Dairy Cow Inn, 51 Northgate (B)
199. Devonshire Hotel, 53 Northgate (F)
200. Red Lion Inn, 55 Northgate (F)
201. Mason's Arms, 90 Northgate (F)
202. Bull & Butcher Inn, 59 Northgate (F)
203. Clifton Arms, 32 Queen Street (F)
204. Brushmakers Arms, 23, 25 Queen Street (B)
205. Industrious Bee, 29 Duke Street (B)
206. General Wolfe Inn, 69 Northgate (F)
207. Grapes Inn, 93 King William Street and 108 Northgate (F)
208. Sawley Abbey, 38, 40 Blakey Moor (B)
209. Golden Ball, 46 Blakey Moor (F)
210. Jubilee Hotel, 29 Blakey Moor (F)
211. Peel Hotel, 1 Barton Street and 6 Cardwell Place (F)

212. Reed Hotel, 11 St. Paul Street (F)
213. Syklark Inn, 4 & 6 Back Blakey Street and Winter Street (B)
214. St. George's Inn, 49 Winter Street (F)
215. Green Vine Inn, 17, 19 Winter Street (B)
216. Hope Inn, 10, 12 Hope Street (B)
217. Bank Hotel, 7 Hope Street (F)
218. Pack Horse, 13 Blakey Street (B)
219. Gardener's Arms, 38, 40 Blakey Street (B)
220. Rock of Gibraltar, 58, 60 Blakey Street (B)
221. Old Red Lion Hotel, 59 Snig Brook (F)
222. Nightingale Inn, 12 Nightingale Street (F)
223. Snig Brook Tavern, 45 Snig Brook (B)
224. Shoulder of Mutton Inn, 26 Snig Brook (F)
225. Barleymow Inn, 27, 29 Snig Brook (B)
226. Farmers Arms, 13 Barley Lane (B)
227. Brewers Arms, 17, 19 St. Paul Street (B)
228. Old Water Mill, 9 St. Paul Street (B)
229. Bull's Head Inn, 59 Blakey Moor (F)
230. Vulcan Inn, 19 Nab Lane (F)
231. Poet's Corner, 2 Bradshaw Street (B)
232. Mechanics' Arms, 39 Nab Lane (B)
233. White Hart Inn, 6 Nab Lane (F)
234. Park Inn, 85 Montague Street (F)
235. Hornby's Arms, 79 Montague Street (F)
236. Spinners' Arms, 2 Jackson Street and 12 Bradshaw Street (B)
237. Rose Bud Inn, 26 Bradshaw Street (B)
238. Duke of York, 56 Montague Street (B)
239. Woodlark Inn, 51 Montague Street (B)
240. Friends' Home, 65 Montague Street & 1 Greaves Street (B)
241. Vine Inn, 41 Montague Street (F)
242. Fielden's Arms, 42 Leyland Street and 51 Adelaide Street (F)
243. Falcon Inn, 50 Montague Street (F)
244. Prince Albert, 74 Fielden Street (B)
245. Dyers' Arms, 16 Greaves Street (B)
246. Bradshaw Arms Hotel, 76 Leyland Street and 25 Dugdale Street (F)
247. Good Samaritan, 46, 48 Greaves Street (B)
248. Nosegay Tavern, 53 Leyland Street and 57 Greaves Street (B)
249. Neptune Hotel, 68 Leyland Street (F)
250. Horse and Jockey, 58 Mary Ann Street (B)
251. Sir Robert Peel, 41 Leyland Street and 41, 43 Mary Ann Street (B)

252. Brewery Inn, 33 Mary Ann Street (B)
253. Bee Hive Inn, 13 Mary Ann Street (F)
254. Stokers' Arms, 14, 16 Addison Street (B)
255. Nile Cottage, 117, 119 Greaves Street and 28 Addison Street (B)
256. Pineapple Inn, 83 Johnston Street (F)
257. Friendship Tavern, 64 Addison Street and 1 Cowell Street (B)
258. Great Eastern, 8 Cowell Street (B)
259. Whitehead's Arms Inn, 58 Cowell Street (F)
260. Prince of Wales Hotel, 97 Montague Street (F)
261. Royal Duke Inn, 14 Johnston Street (F)
262. Earl of Derby Inn, 58 Greaves Street (F)
263. Off License, 1 Whitehead Street
264. Claremont Hotel, 49 Sarah Ellen Street and 164 Addison Street (F)
265. Imperial Inn, 25 Sarah Ellen Street (F)
266. Off License, 31 Bromley Street and 79 Sarah Ellen Street
267. Cheetham Arms, 17 Lawrence Street (F)
268. Hindles Arms, 68 Wensley Street and 2 Lawrence Street (B)
269. Lancashire Lad, 70, 72 Wensley Street (B)
270. Lion Hotel, 29 Wensley Street (F)
271. Forrest Arms, 67 Wensley Street (F)
272. White Hart Inn, 162 Wensley Street (F)
273. Boar's Head, 131 Wensley Street (B)
274. Ouzehead Inn, 39 Long Row (F)
275. Fox and Grapes Inn, 3 Limefield (F)
276. Off-License, 22 Leamington Street
277. Leamington Hotel, 1 Cheltenham Street (F)
278. Alexandra Hotel, 29 Duke's Brow (F)
279. Gibraltar Inn, 1 Gibraltar Street (F)
280. Quarryman's Arms, 109 Duke's Brow (B)
281. Dog Inn, Revidge Road (B)
282. West View Inn, 20 Revidge Road (F)
283. Yew Tree Inn, 1 Beardwood (F)
284. Clarence Hotel, 2 and 4 Lord Street (F)
285. St. Leger Hotel, 19 King William Street (F)
286. Queen's Hotel, 16 Town Hall Street (F)
287. Exchange Hotel, 59, 61 King William Street (F)
288. Off License, 9 Town Hall Street
289. Off License, Exchange Buildings
290. Crown Hotel, 38 and 40 Victoria Street (F)
291. Garrick's Head, 7 Ainsworth Street (B)
292. Victoria Inn, 11 Cort Street (F)
293. Haymarket Tavern, 1 and 3 Cort Street (F)
294. Prince Albert Hotel, 36, 38 Ainsworth Street (F)

295. Grosvenor Hotel, Shorrock Fold and Lord Street (F)
296. New Inn, 3, 5 Victoria Street (F)
297. Star Inn, 7 Shorrock Fold (F)
298. Golden Lion Hotel, 51 Church Street (F)
299. Bay Horse Hotel, 1 Salford (F)
300. Lord Nelson Inn, 11 Salford (F)
301. Farmer's Boy Arms, 13 Water Street (B)
302. Welcome Inn, 23 Penny Street (B)
303. The Shamrock, 39 Penny Street (B)
304. Britannia Inn, 51, 53 Penny Street (F)
305. Pheasant Inn, 55, 57 Penny Street (B)
306. Fleece Inn, 24 Penny Street (F)
307. Smiths' Arms, 57 Water Street (B)
308. Regent Hotel, 14, 16 Old Chapel Street (F)
309. Boar's Head, 9 Old Chapel Street (F)
310. Spread Eagle, 4 Cable Street (F)
311. Plough Inn, 121 Penny Street (F)
312. Anchor Inn, 2 Syke Street (B)
313. Albion Hotel, 3 and 5 Syke Street (F)
314. Great Britain, 12, 14 Syke Street (B)
315. Ireland's Glory, 55, 57 Moor Street (B)
316. Gladstone Hotel, 41 Moor Street (F)
317. Duke of Connaught, 83 Moor Street (B)
318. Uncle Tom's Cabin, 97, 99 Moor Street (B)
319. Coach and Horses, 21 Larkhill Street (B)
320. Waterloo Inn, 86 Penny Street (F)
321. Larkhill Tavern, 1 Larkhill Street (B)
322. Ship Inn, 151 Penny Street and 48 Brown Street (B)
323. Old House at Home, 8 Larkhill (B)
324. Trinity Tavern, 24 Mount Pleasant (B)
325. Off-license, 20 Regent Street and 70 John Street
326. Larkhill Inn, 33 Larkhill (F)
327. Unicorn Hotel, 66 Mount Pleasant (F)
328. Off-license, 96 Larkhill
329. Albion Hotel, 17 Smithies Street (F)
330. Primrose Inn, 39 Primrose Bank (F)
331. Flowing Jug, 28 Birley Street (B)
332. Fisher's Arms, 83 Birley Street (F)
333. Dutton's Arms, 65, 67 Birley Street (B)
334. Daisyfield Tavern, 37, 39 Union Buildings (B)
335. Plantation Tavern, 43 Moss Street (B)
336. Hare and Hounds, 112 Union Buildings (B)
337. Brown Cow, 71 Union Buildings (B)

338. Cromwell Hotel, 28 Peter Street (F)
339. Florence Hotel, 149 Moss Street (F)
340. Royal Exchange Hotel, 20 Swarbrick Street (F)
341. Moss Street Tavern, 41 Moss Street (B)
342. Hornby's Arms, 22 Union Buildings (B)
343. Daisyfield Hotel, 46 Whalley Old Road (F)
344. Toll Bar Inn, 2 and 4 Whalley Old Road (B)
345. St. Alban's Tavern, 8 Birley Street (B)
346. Cotton Tree Inn, 13 Birley Street (F)
347. Beech Tree Inn, 13 Cob Wall (B)
348. Plane Tree Inn, 23 Cob Wall (F)
349. Off-license, 40 Plane Street
350. Bastwell Hotel, 83 Whalley New Road (F)
351. Off-license, 182 Whalley New Road
352. Stanley Arms, 2 and 4 Pemberton Street (F)
353. Royal Oak, 1 and 2 Pleckgate (B)
354. Knowles Arms, 23 Further Wilworth (F)
355. Sportsman's Arms, Four Lane Ends (B)
356. Jolly Dragoon, 117 Four Lane Ends (F)
357. Hare and Hounds, 5 Lanack (F)
358. Hole-i'th'-Wall Inn, 184 Hole-i'th'-Wall (F)
359. Corporation Park Hotel, Revidge Road (F)
360. Off License, 180 Shear Brow
361. Brown Cow, 1 Top Farm (B)
362. Carlton Hotel, 48 Shear Brown (F)
363. Swan Hotel, 22 Whalley Range (F)
364. Anchor Hotel, 60 London Road (F)
365. Whalley Range Inn, 48 Whalley Range (F)
366. Gardeners' Arms, 30 Whalley Range (F)
367. Off license, 116 Randal Street
368. Balaclava Inn, 27 Watson's Buildings and 1 Charlotte Street (F)
369. Confectioner's Shop, 78 Victoria Street (B)
370. Off-license, 59 Victoria Street
371. Leopard's Head, 2 Lime Street (F)
372. Derby's Arms, 1 Limbrick (B)
373. Sir Charles Napier, 12 Limbrick (F)
374. Old Arm Chair, 32 Tontine Street (B)
375. Richmond Inn, 50 Tontine Street (F)
376. Hindle's Arms Inn, 7 Richmond Hill (F)
377. The Rock, 1 Bolton's Court (B)
378. Dog and Partridge, 15, 17 James Street (B)
379. Royal, 70 Victoria Street (F)
380. Tam O'Shanter, 9 Brookhouse Lane (B)

381. Brookhouse Tavern, 10 Brookhouse Lane (B)
382. Craven Heifer Inn, 1, 3 Whalley New Road (F)
383. Off License, 17 Butler Street
384. Borough Arms Hotel, 8 Tacketts Street and 17 Exchange Street (F)
385. St. John's Tavern, 1 Union Street (F)
386. Chandlers' Arms, 20 Union Street (B)
387. Royal Archers' Arms, 4 Swallow Street and 2 Hilton Street (B)
388. Off License, 89 James Street
389. Stoker's Arms, 73 Darwen Street (B)
390. Woodman Inn, 1 Bridge Street (F)
391. Merchants Hotel, 43, 45 Darwen Street (F)
392. Queen's Head Inn, 17 Darwen Street (F)
393. Darwen and County Arms, 9 and 11 Darwen Street (F)
394. Legs of Man, 1, 3, 5 Darwen Street (F)
395. Old Bull Hotel, 18 Church Street (F)
396. Off License, 22, 24 Church Street (shop)
397. White Bull Hotel, 62 Church Street (F)
398. Old White Bull Inn, 8 Salford (F)
399. Peel Arms Hotel, 39 Salford (F)
400. Royal Oak, 38 Salford (B)
401. Beehive Inn, 8 High Street (B)
402. Dolphin Hotel, 6 Mount Street (F)
403. Star and Garter Hotel, 45 Railway Road (F)
404. Adelphi Hotel, 33 Railway Road (F)
405. Oak Tavern Inn, 9 Vicar Street (B)
406. Veteran Inn, 93 Salford (F)
407. Bowling Green Inn, 33 Eanam and 68, 70 Syke Street (F)
408. New Drop, 16, 18, 20 Syke Street (B)
409. Ward's Hotel, 29 Syke Street (F)
410. Bay Horse Inn, 72 Moor Street (B)
411. Rose Bud Inn, 42 Larkhill Street (B)
412. Commercial Inn, 110 Moor Street (B)
413. White Lion, 41, 43 Larkhill Street (B)
414. Cross Guns, 51 Larkhill Street (B)
415. Anglers' Arms, 89, 91 Cleaver Street (B)
416. Off license, 119 Cleaver Street
417. Foundry Arms, 139 Cleaver Street (F)
418. Boat House Inn, 24 Eanam (F)
419. Friendship Tavern, 30, 32 Eanam (B)
420. Rock Inn, 51 Eanam (F)
421. Packet House, 1 and 3 Bancroft Street (B)
422. Canal Tavern, 67 Eanam, 2 & 4, Bancroft Street (B)
423. Navigation Inn, 69 Eanam (F)

424. Army and Navy Hotel, 145 Birley Street (F)
425. Pelican Inn, 123 Birley Street (F)
426. Salisbury Hotel, 78 Peter Street (F)
427. Globe Inn, 2, 4 Higher Eanam (F)
428. Millstone Tavern, 11, 13 Higher Eanam (B)
429. Brewer's Arms, 19 Higher Eanam (B)
430. Fox and Goose Inn, 35A Higher Eanam (F)
431. Rose and Crown Inn, 4 Copy Nook (F)
432. Albert Inn, 17 Copy Nook (B)
433. Pendle Tavern, 7 Pendle Street (B)
434. Copy Nook Inn, 27 Copy Nook (B)
435. Royal Oak, 68 Copy Nook (B)
436. Hopwood Arms, 3 Bottomgate (F)
437. Thorn Inn, 42 Bottomgate (F)
438. Black Stag, 13 Bottomgate (F)
439. Ship Inn, 23, 25 Bottomgate (B)
440. Spectator Inn, 60 Bottomgate (B)
441. Isle of St. Helena, 62 Bottomgate (B)
442. Royal George, 82 Bottomgate (B)
443. Oddfellows Arms, 61 Bottomgate (B)
444. Pipemaker's Arms, 91 Bottomgate (F)
445. Carter's Arms, 117 Bottomgate (B)
446. Forresters Arms, 44 Woolwich Street (F)
447. Ordnance Inn, 1 Woolwich Street (F)
448. Prince of Wales Inn, 90 Harwood Street (F)
449. Recreation Inn, 20 Harwood Street (B)
450. Duke of Edinburgh, 3 Crabtree Street (F)
451. Greenbank Hotel, 140 Harwood Street (F)
452. Royal Edward, 146 Harwood Street (F)
453. Rose and Thistle Inn, 148 Harwood Street (F)
454. Little Harwood Hotel, 181 Whalley Old Road (F)
455. Off License, 2, 4 Elm Street and Bey Street
456. Thwaite's Arms, 318 Whalley New Road (F)
457. Cemetery Hotel, Whalley New Road (F)
458. Rising Sun, 9 Bull's Head, Whalley New Road (B)
459. Bull's Head Inn, Whalley New Road (F)
460. Royal Oak, 32, 34 Furthergate (B)
461. Hare and Hounds Inn, 47, 49 Furthergate (B)
462. Hop Bine Inn, 58 Furthergate (B)
463. Wellington Inn, 57 Furthergate (F)
464. Grapes Inn, 15, 17 Burnley Road (B)
465. Printers' Arms, 15 Accrington Road (F)
466. Gardners' Arms, 19 Accrington Road (B)

467. Off-license, 87, 89 Burnley Road
468. Hole House Inn, 137 Burnley Road (F)
469. Red Lion Inn, 21 Whitebirk (F)
470. Intack Inn, 357 Accrington Road (F)
471. Face i'th' Brow, 98 Accrington Road (B)
472. Fountain Inn, Accrington Road (F)
473. Crescent Hotel, Intack Crescent (F)
474. Forrester's Arms, 4 Shadsworth (F)
475. Plantation Tavern, 3 Knuzden Brook (B)
476. Queen's Hotel, 185 Audley Range (F)
477. Audley Range Hotel, 149 Audley Range (F)
478. Lord Howard Arms Hotel, 93 Audley Range (F)
479. Of License, 132 Chester Street
480. Brunswick Hotel, 225 Higher Audley Street (F)
481. Golden Sceptre Hotel, 8 Scotland Road (F)
482. Audley Bowling Green Inn, 40 Scotland Road (F)
483. Scotland Road Hotel, 62, 64 Scotland Road (F)
484. Maysons' Arms, 23 Audley Lane (F)
485. Mitre Inn, 72 William Hopwood Street (F)
486. Off-license, 45 Addington Street
487. Lord Clyde Hotel, 31 Audley Street (F)
488. Clover Hotel, 34 Audley Lane (F)
489. Canterbury Hotel, 76 Withers Street (F)
490. Walpole Hotel, 50 Withers Street (F)
491. Wellington Hotel, 153 Higher Audley Street (F)
492. Cicely Bridge Inn, 125, 127 Higher Audley Street (F)
493. Cicely Hole Hotel, 109, 111 Higher Audley Street (F)
494. Off License, 30, 32 Higher Audley Street
495. Audley Arms, 37 Higher Audley Street (F)

---

**Brewers (Wholesale).**

Beardsworth & Whalley, Little Harwood brewery
Blackburn Brewery Co., Ltd., Higher Eanam ; Charles Henry Ashton, manager and secretary
Bourn Thos., Crown brewery, Canterbury street
Cunningham J. & Co., Snig Brook brewery
Dutton & Co., Salford brewery
Green & Whalley, Albert brewery, Cort st

**HOLDEN RICHARD, New brewery, 81 Bolton road**

**SHAW H. & Co., Salford New brewery** (See Advt.)

Smith William, Dukes street and 9 Town Hall street
Thwaites Daniel & Co., Eanam brewery
Whewell Thomas, Victoria brewery, Adelaide street

---

**Botanic Beer Makers.**

Dodd R. & Co., 237 Audley range
Greenwood Henry, 14, 16 Myrtle street
Lucas William, 58 Belgrave street
Waddington J. E., 6 Audley range
Wilding James, 10 Warwick street

---